Volleyball Skills & Drills

Jim Bertoli

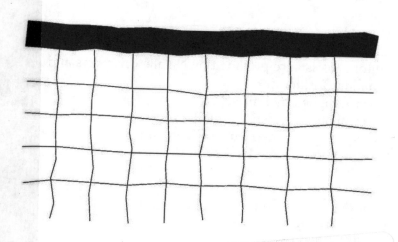

Wish
PUBLISHING

...blishing
Indiana
...ing.com

LCCN: 2003112650

Edited by Kim Heusel
Editorial assistance provided by Natalie Chambers and Amanda Burkhardt
Cover designed by Phil Velikan
Cover photo provided by Jim Bertoli
Interior diagrams by Debbie Oldenburg
Interior photography by Joseph C. Garza
Model: Alison Pinkston

Printed in the United States of America
10 9 8 7 6 5 4 3 2 1

Published in the United States by
Wish Publishing
P.O. Box 10337
Terre Haute, IN 47801, USA
www.wishpublishing.com

Distributed in the United States by
Cardinal Publishers Group
7301 Georgetown Road, Suite 118
Indianapolis, Indiana 46268
www.cardinalpub.com

Table of Contents

Things to Know Before We Start

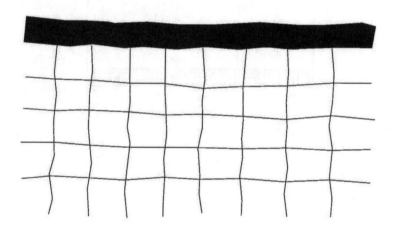

Zones of Opponents Court

Above you will find the six zones of the opponent's court. These zones will be referred to when talking about serving, defense and attack.

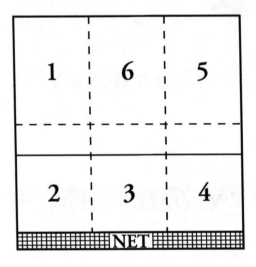

Zones of the Net & Set Definition

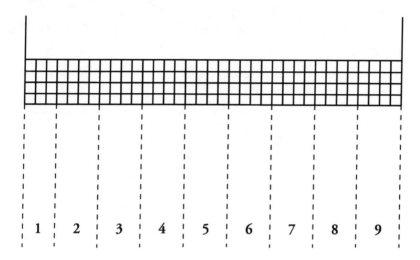

Zones of the Net

These attack lanes are used as reference points along the net for the purposes of attack and blocking. Zone six is the area at the net that you want all of your passes and digs to go to in order to run your offense. The odd numbered zones are typically used as attack lanes while the even numbered lanes can be used as reference points along the net for blocking locations.

Set Definition

"1" is in the 5 zone, 1 foot above the net at its peak

"2" is in the 5 zone, 2 feet above the net at its peak

"3" is in the 3 zone, 1 foot above the net at its peak

"4" is in the 1 zone, four feet above the net at its peak

"5" is in the 1 zone, five feet above the net at its peak

"6" is in the 7 zone, one foot above the net at its peak

"7"is in the 8 zone, two feet above the net at its peak

"8"is in the 9 zone, 3 feet above the net at its peak

"9" is in the 9 zone, 4 feet above the net at its peak

"A" is a back row attack set to the left back at the 3 meter line

"B" is a back row attack set to the middle back at the 3 meter line

"C" is a back row attack set to the right back at the 3 meter line

Defenses

White Defense, (Man Back or Deep Six)

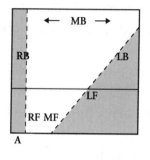

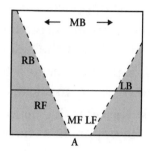

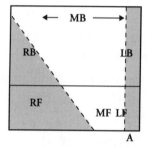

Black Defense, (Modified Rotational)

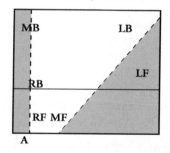

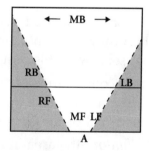

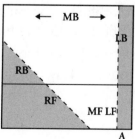

A = attacker
RF = right front
MF = middle front
LF = left front

RB = right back
MB = middle back
LB = left back

Terminology

Ace: also known as a service ace, is a ball that is served that the opponent can not make a second contact.

Antenna: vertical rod on the outside edge of the net aligned just outside of the sidelines.

Assist: a pass or set to a teammate who attacks the ball and it results in a kill.

Attack: the offensive action of one team to place the ball in the opponent's court.

Attacker: a player who is attempting to terminate a set by hitting it into the opponent's court.

Attack Line: the lines on the court that are located three meters from the center line on each side of the court.

Back Row Attack: an attack in which a back row player jumps from behind the attack line and attacks the ball into the opponent's court.

Balancing the Court: when players cover areas of the court that are left open by a teammate that has just made a play.

Be balanced: term used to be sure that a player is stable when they are contacting the ball while passing, setting, serving or blocking.

Block: the combination of one, two or three front row players that jump at the net in an attempt to intercept the spiked ball of the opponent.

Block Shadow-the area in the court behind the block that is taken out by the block. The majority of your floor defenders should be outside the block shadow.

Close the block: term used with blockers referring to the blocker that is moving towards a teammate to help block an attack.

Cut Shot: when a player attacks or spikes the ball from an outside hitting position crosscourt to the opponent's far court area.

Deep Six: a defensive system also known as the "man back" defense where the player who is located in the 6 zone plays their defense in the middle back area of the court.

Double Hit or Double Contact: successive hits by the same player. Also referred to as multiple contacts.

Double Quick: a play set where two attackers approach the setter, one in front and one behind for first tempo sets at the same time.

Down Ball: a ball that is attacked by a player who remains on the floor and uses the upper body technique of a spike to attack the ball into the opponent's court.

Drive the legs: term used referring the forward motion of a passer's legs towards target.

First tempo sets: sets that are typically only one foot or less above the net at it peak. First tempo sets are usually hit by middle hitters or right side attackers.

Five-One Offense: an offensive system that incorporates one individual that sets and five individuals that are attackers.

Floater: a serve with no spin that has an erratic flight path.

Free Ball: a ball that is returned across the net with a forearm or overhead pass rather than a spike.

Front the Hitter: the action of a blocker to place themselves at a spot at the net that intersects the angle of the attacker.

*Jump Serve-*a serve where the server incorporates an attack approach while serving.

Kill: a successful attack attempt that hits the opponent's floor or is deflected off the opponent's player that results in a point.

Libero: designated back row player who can replace any other player in a back row position. He or she can not serve or attack the ball. The libero wears a jersey of a contrasting color to that of their team.

Line Shot: an attacked ball hit down the opponent's sideline that is closest to the attacker.

Loaded Legs: phrase that describes the proper flexion in the players knee for their block start stance, for movement and when exploding from the floor.

Offside Blocker: the player in the front row that is not blocking and that pulls off the net to play floor defense.

Overhead Pass: a pass made with both hands open, controlled by the fingers, also known as a "set".

Overlap: a foul committed when a player is out of rotation when the ball is served.

Pancake: an emergency defensive technique where the player places their hand flat on the floor and the ball rebounds off the back of their hand.

Pass: the first contact, which involves using the forearms to contact the ball towards the setter.

Pepper: a warm up drill involving two players that involves attacking, digging and setting between the players.

Pin to Pin: refers to the antenna used on the net and an offensive strategy where your setter alternates sets from one pin to the other pin to stretch out, and confuse the opponent's blockers.

Pre-Hop: defensive prep step where the defenders slightly widen their stance to get lower and to get their weight forward before the attacker starts their arm swing.

Press over the net: phrase used to describe the blockers penetrating their hands over the net, pushing or pressing them forward.

Rally Scoring: scoring format that involves every rally resulting in a point for the winner of the rally.

Read Defense: when the defenders anticipate and react to the opponent's movement and defend accordingly.

Ready Position: the flexed posture a player assumes before moving to perform a skill and contact the ball.

Roof: when the blocker blocks an attack attempt and the ball is propelled straight down into the opponent's court.

Rotation: the clockwise movement of players around the court and through the serving position following a side out.

Roll Shot: a ball that is attacked by a player, who uses the proper attack approach, but hits an off speed attack by slowing down the arm swing.

Screening: the illegal placement of blockers at the net to impair the vision of the passers when serving.

Seal the net: phrase used to describe the blockers arms tight to the net when blocking.

Serve: the act of attacking the ball to put it into play in the opponent's court.

Set: the act of passing the ball to a teammate for them to attack the ball into the opponent's court.

Second tempo sets: sets that are about two feet above the net at their peak.

Side Out: when the team that receives serve wins the rally.

Six Packed: phrase used to describe a player getting hit in the face by an attack.

Six-Two Offense: an offense system that involves two individuals setting the ball and six individuals attacking the ball. The setter is always coming from the back court to set three attackers in every rotation.

Slide: an attack approach that incorporates a one foot take off similar to a basketball lay up.

Soft Block: a blocking technique where the blockers bend their hands back to create a surface for the ball to be deflected back into play. Used by shorter blockers or by blockers who have left the floor late while blocking.

Spike: a ball contacted with force into the opponent's court with the intent to terminate the play with a kill.

Staggered Stance: refers to the stance of a passer or defender where the right foot is slightly in front of the left foot to enable the passer or defender to move from the stance and to drive the ball forward to their target.

Sticking the pass: the term used to describe a passer being balanced and stationary at the point of contact with their platform to target

Stuff Block: a ball that is deflected back into the attacking team's court by the block for a point, or side out.

Target Area: the desired area toward which a pass is directed. Normally the target area is the setter, or the right front area. Zone 6 of the 9 along the net.

Tip: to attack the ball into the opponent's court with an open hand using an off speed shot.

Tool Shot: to attack the ball and deflect it off of the opponent's block.

Transition: the movement of a player or the team from offense to defense, defense to offense or passing to attack.

Turning the block to 3/6: the phrase used to describe the angle of the blocker's hands towards the center of the opponent's court when blocking.

"W" for winners, not "L" for losers: phrase used to describe the proper hand positioning in their block start

stance and while blocking. The letters describe the formation of the player's fingers.

Zones: a numbering system used to designate the placement of sets, passes, attacks, serves, players, offensive or defensive systems.

1

Warm Up Drills & Ball Control

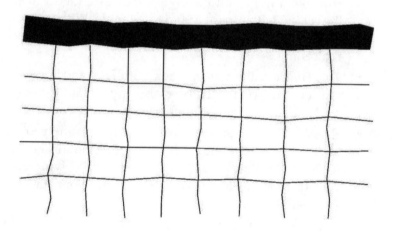

Core

We do "core" on a daily basis due to the importance of making the athlete's core muscle group strong. The core muscle groups consist of the lower back area, the stomach and abdominal area. Strength in these areas is vital to successfully performing all volleyball skills. We do our core workout after the athletes have done their stretching. We typically use five of these exercises on a daily basis. Here is a list of the different core exercises that you can use:

- *Legs Straight Out:* Lie flat on back with legs extended on the ground combined with abdominal crunch motion.

- *Legs Crossed:* Lie flat on back with legs crossed on the ground combined with an abdominal crunch motion.

- *Hip-ups:* Lie flat on back with legs extended toward the ceiling with hips at a 90-degree angle. Without rocking legs, bring hips off the ground, forcing legs toward the ceiling.

- *Toe Touches:* Lie flat on back with legs and arms extended toward the ceiling and hips at a 90-degree angle. Using an abdominal crunch, touch your toes.

- *Regular:* Lie flat on back with feet flat on the ground and hands behind your head; use an abdominal crunch to slowly lift the shoulders off the ground driving your chin toward the ceiling and contracting your navel to your spine.

- *V-Crunches:* Lie flat on back with legs extended off the ground in a V shape, hips at a 45-degree angle combined with an abdominal crunch.

- *Roaches:* Lie flat on back with legs extended off of ground in a V shape and hips at a 45-degree angle. Using the arms, reach between legs toward heels.

- *Heel Touches:* Feet flat on the ground, shoulders off the ground, arms parallel with the ground; use side abdominals to touch the opposite heel. Repeat on other side.

- *Alternate Toe Touches:* Lie flat on back with arms extended toward the ceiling with hips at a 90-degree angle. Using an abdominal crunch, touch opposite hand to opposite foot. Repeat on other side.

- *Twisties:* Balanced on tailbone with feet off the ground, rotate shoulders so the opposite hand touches the floor. Repeat on other side.

- *Bicycles:* Lie flat on back with legs extended, parallel to the floor. Bring one knee close to the body while simultaneously using an abdominal crunch to meet that knee with the opposite elbow. Repeat on the other side.

- *Leg Circles:* Lie flat on back with legs extended 3 to 5 inches off the floor, hand under your tailbone, and head off of the floor; create small circles with your toes. Repeat in the opposite direction.

- *Scissors:* Lie flat on back with legs extended 6 to 7 inches off the floor, hands under your tailbone, and head off of floor; bring one leg up toward the ceiling (not exceeding 45 degrees). In a swift motion alternate legs.

- *Side Scissors:* Lie flat on back keeping legs extended 6 to 7 inches off the floor in a V shape, hands under your tailbone, and head off the floor. Crisscross legs in a swift motion.

- *Front Holds:* With arms at a 90-degree angle, elbows and toes on the floor, and head up, hold the body off of the floor with back, hips, and knees straight for a certain amount of time.

- *Side Holds:* Balanced on one hand and the side of one foot, hold the body off of floor with back, hips, and knees straight for a certain amount of time. It may help balance to extend unused arm into the air.

- *Reverse Trunk Twist:* Lie flat on back with arms extended on the floor at your sides and hips and knees at a 90-degree angle; lower knees to one side and return to starting position, keeping your shoulders on the ground. Repeat on the other side.

- *Side Crunches:* Lie on one side with knees and hips at a 45-degree angle, shoulders on the ground, and hands behind your head. With top leg 3 to 4 inches off the bottom leg, use an abdominal crunch to bring opposite elbow toward hip.

- *Opposite Elbow/Opposite Knee:* Lie flat on back with hands behind head and one foot on the ground. With the other leg, place the angle on the grounded leg's knee. Using an abdominal crunch, bring the opposite elbow to the nongrounded knee.

- *Block Holds:* Lie on back with arms and legs extended on the ground creating a 180-degree angle with body. Contract body so that shoulders and legs are off the ground in blocking form for a certain amount of time.

- *Sit-ups:* Lie flat on back with feet on the ground and hands behind head. Using an abdominal crunch, lift body off the ground so that elbows can touch the knees.

- *Fives:* Lie flat on back with feet on the floor and hands behind head. Using an abdominal crunch, contract 5 times bringing shoulders off the ground, 5 times with hips at a 45-degree angle, and 5 times touching your elbows to your knees. Repeat.

- *Jackknife:* Lie flat on back with arms and legs extended on the floor creating a 180-degree angle with the body. Keeping arms above head and legs straight, contract body so that you balance on your tailbone and touch your toes.

- *Leg Extension:* Lie flat on back with arms under tailbone and legs extended on ground. Keeping shoulders on ground bring straight legs off the ground not exceeding 45-degree angle.

- *Partner abs/straight and angle:* Lie flat on back with a partner standing overhead. Bring legs toward the ceiling, bending hips at a 90-degree angle. It may help to stabilize yourself by grabbing onto partner's ankles. Partner will then push legs toward the floor. Keeping legs straight and back on the floor, allow your legs to come close to the floor and then quickly return to the starting position. Legs may be pushed straight down or at an angle.

- *Superman:* Lie on stomach. Keeping head up, raise arms, shoulders, and knees off the floor by contracting back muscles.

- *Superman/just arms:* Lie on stomach. Keeping head up, raise arms and shoulders off the floor by contracting back muscles.

- *Superman/opposite arm/opposite leg:* Lie on stomach. Keeping head up, raise right arm and left leg off the floor by contracting back muscles. Repeat with left arm and right leg.

- *Bridges:* On hands and knees, extend right leg and left arm, keeping back straight. Repeat with left leg and right arm.

Full-Court Arm Warm-Up

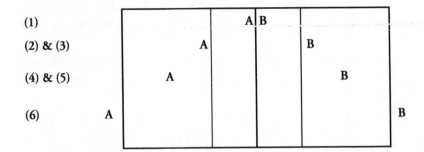

This arm warm-up drill utilizes the court and the net to make sure that your athletes are using the proper wrist action, arm swing, arm extension, body positioning, and technique for attacking/spiking.

(1) **Wrist Snaps at Net:** The first stage of this progression is to loosen, or warm up, the wrist and to promote proper hand contact on the ball. Two players are located at the net, one on each side of the net facing each other. One ball per group of two players is needed. In this stage, each player will hit five balls with each hand, first with the dominant hand, then with the nondominant hand. The player holds the ball in one hand in front of the hitting hand. The elbow of the hitting hand should be tight to the side of the body with the hand pulled up in front of the shoulder, the wrist cocked back and hand spread open. The player tosses the ball up slightly and simply snaps the wrist downward on to the ball so that the ball bounces off the centerline of the court and rebounds up to the partner. The partner then does the same back to the other person. Remember, five reps with each hand

(2) **Two-Arm Overhead Toss at the Attack Line:** The next progression is to have the player move backward to the area just behind the attack line. From there, the player throws the ball to her partner by using a two-hand overhead toss over the net. Be sure that the play-

ers are getting a full extension at release and that they are taking a small step forward with their right foot. Five tosses per player are enough at this stage.

(3) One-Arm Overhead Toss: Next, the players will throw the ball to their partners five times using their nondominant hand first and then do 10 throws with their dominant hand. Make sure the athlete's elbow is high throughout the throwing motion.

(4) Down Ball: The next progression involves the players moving back so they are 6 meters from the net, or a little over halfway between the attack line and the end line. From this point the players should underhand-toss the ball with two hands in front of their dominant arm and hit a roll shot over the net to their partners. We want the players to toss with two hands so they can simulate the arm action of bringing both arms up in the air and then executing the correct upper-body movement. Be sure that the players are tossing the ball forward in front of their hitting shoulders. Once players have contacted five roll shots they move on to the next progression.

(5) Centerline Bounce Attack at ¾-Court: At this point, the players are tossing the ball in a similar fashion to the previous progression, but they are making a high contact and with a strong wrist snap so that the ball is hitting near the centerline of the court and bouncing to their partners. If the players are using the correct technique they will be able to place the ball near the centerline with their attack. If they are contacting the ball too far in front of their body the ball will bounce well in front of the centerline on their side of the net and will bounce over the net instead of under the net. If the players contact the ball too far behind them, the ball will bounce into the net. After players successfully attack five balls they should move on to the last progression of the drill.

(6) Serving from End line: The last progression involves players serving the ball from behind the end line suc-

cessfully five times each. The previous steps in the progression actually help to train the players' arms to serve the ball more proficiently. Be sure to emphasize proper technique here and don't let the athletes revert to bad habits that they may have developed in their serving technique in the past.

Pepper

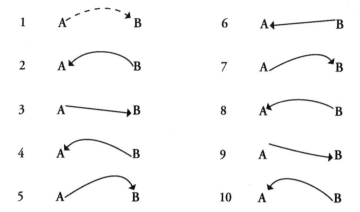

The classic volleyball warm-up drill of pepper is often underappreciated and often done improperly. The drill was designed to have players warm up, but also to concentrate on performing the skills of attack, digging, and setting the ball in preparation for competing. Many times players use improper technique and do not put forth the effort they should in this ball-control drill. This drill consists of having two players using one ball to work on their ball-control skills of digging, setting, and attacking. In the above diagram, player A and player B are "peppering." The progression of the drill is:

1. Player A tosses the ball to B.

2. Player B forearm-passes the ball back to A.

3. Player A then attacks the ball with a down ball at B.

4. Player B digs the ball back to A.

5. Player A then sets the ball to B.

6. Player B attacks the ball at A.

7. Player A digs the ball back to B.

8. Player B sets the ball back to A.

9. Player A attacks the ball at B.

10. Player B digs the ball back to A.

Be sure to emphasize proper technique while your athletes are performing all of the skills. Have them concentrate on their arm swing when attacking, their pre-hop on the defense, and moving their feet and getting square to target on their overhead pass.

Double-Dig Pepper

We came up with this variation of traditional pepper to address a problem that we are having with our athletes keeping their weight forward in their defensive stance. We asked our athletes to modify their normal pepper routine of dig-set-attack to dig-dig-set, attack-attack. Player "A" digs a hard driven attack by player "B" and then must dig a second ball from her defensive stance. The second ball should be an off-speed shot. Make sure that your athletes aren't changing their defensive stances between the balls that they are digging.

Queen of the Court

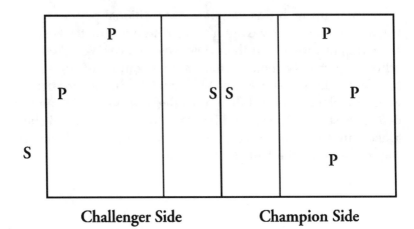

Challenger Side   **Champion Side**

This is a drill that most teams use and is very popular with the athletes. I prefer to conduct this drill using a quads format or four-on-four. In using a quad format, it resembles the backcourt defense that most teams utilize with a right-back, middle-back, and left-back defender. We split up our team for this drill in a unique way. As our players are lined up on the end line, we ask them to line up in alphabetical order by some personal theme such as their middle name, first pet's name, first boyfriend's name, mother's maiden name, etc. The athletes have a lot of fun with it and it gets them excited to play. Once we have determined the teams, one team is placed on the "champion" side of the net. The other teams are lined up on the challenger side of the court; the team on this side will serve the ball at all times. We typically play this drill to 10 points, and the only way a team can score is to win a rally while it is on the champion side of the court. The team that wins the rally gets to stay on the champion side or replace the team on that side if it is the challenger. You can have the attackers attacking back row only or at the net. For a more challenging version of this drill, check out the next drill.

Modified Queen of the Court

The same principle applies in this drill as in "Queen of the Court." There is a Challenger side and a Champion side of the court, and a team can only score a point when it wins a rally on the Champion side of the court. The modification is in the scoring format. For points 1 through 5, players can hit on the net, and for points 6 through 10, they must use back-row attack. We don't allow any tips in this drill, but do allow roll shots. You can also adapt the drill to a format that allows the attacker to hit at the net for points 1 through 5, but all the attacks must be off-speed shots and 6 through 10 are back-row attacks using a full swing.

Backcourt Box Shuffle

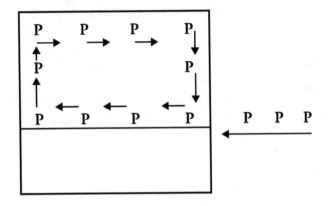

This is a great drill for players of all skill levels. It reinforces the proper footwork and movement for passing and backcourt defense and is also a good conditioning drill. You will be utilizing the backcourt of one side of the court from the attack line to the end line. Start with the players lined up in the left front area of the court at the attack line; facing the opponent's court they will proceed along the attack line with a shuffle step to the right sideline. From there, they will use a backward-shuffle footwork to go from the attack line to the end line and then go to their left along the end line to the left sideline until they get to the left sideline, where they will use a forward-shuffle footwork to get back to their start point. Each player should simulate a passing motion with every shuffle and make sure that she adjusts her body posture and passing platform according to where she is in the court. Be sure that your athletes keep the correct body posture when moving throughout the drill.

Triangle Pepper

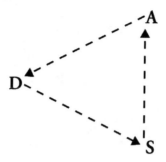

One of the problems with the traditional format of pepper is that it is actually not very game-like. While playing in a game your defenders rarely dig the ball back to where the attack came from, nor do your players usually set a ball back to where the dig came from or attack a ball that is coming straight at them. That is why we like to have our players pepper using a triangle formation using three players. The triangle format helps the players to get the feeling of the ball coming from one direction and having to rebound the ball in a different direction. This drill helps the defenders read a hitter and to rebound the ball to a setter. It also helps your players with their setting since they are receiving the ball from the digger and having to square to their target, the attacker, to set the ball properly. The drill also helps the attacker to move her/his feet and to keep the ball in front of her hitting shoulder and work on placement skills by putting the ball on the defender's arms. Once the defender has successfully dug five or six balls have the players rotate positions.

Inline Pepper

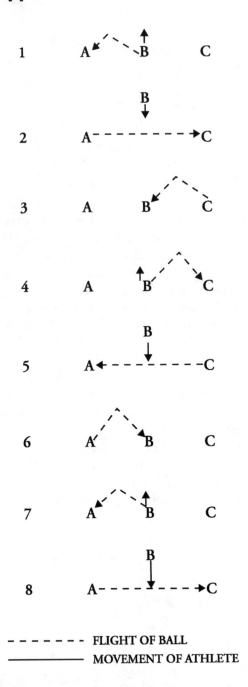

1   A ◄ - - ◄ B   C

2   B ↓
     A - - - - - - - ► C

3   A   B ◄ - - C

4   A   B ↑ - - ► C

5   B ↓
     A ◄ - - - - - C

6   A - - ► B   C

7   A ◄ - - ↑ B   C

8   B ↓
     A - - - - ► C

- - - - - - - FLIGHT OF BALL
————————— MOVEMENT OF ATHLETE

First of all, this drill does not involve roller blades! The "inline" term refers to the fact that the setter in this drill steps in between the attacker and digger to set the ball. This drill involves three players at a time, so split the team up into threes and have them in a straight line as shown in diagram 1. Player A and player C will be attacking and digging the ball throughout the drill, while player B will be setting the ball back to the player that just dug the last ball. Here's a breakdown of the drill by using the diagrams above:

1. The drill is started by having the setter, player B, toss the ball to player A. After tossing the ball, the setter steps out from between players A and C.

2. Player A attacks the ball with a roll shot at player C, who will dig the ball to the area between her and player A. After the spiked ball from player A passes the midpoint, player B should step in between players A and C to get ready to receive the dug ball from player C.

3. Player C has dug the ball to player B.

4. Player B sets the ball back to player C. After the set leaves player B's hands, she steps out from between players A and C.

5. Player C attacks the ball at player A. As the ball passes the midpoint, player B steps between A and C and prepares to receive a dig from player A.

6. Player A digs the ball to player B.

7. Player B sets the ball back to player A and steps out of the middle.

8. Player A attacks the ball at player C and player B steps into the middle after the attack has passed the midpoint.

This progression repeats it self until the setter has satisfied the desired number of sets, or the drill can be played for a predetermined period of time.

Shuffle Snake

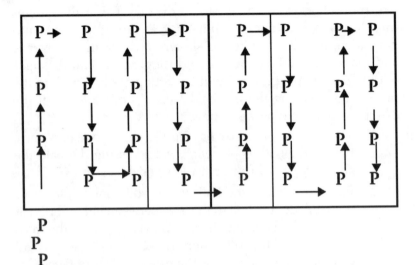

This is a movement drill that will help your athletes with the proper lateral shuffling footwork and forward-to-backward shuffling for passing and defense. Start with the team in the right back area at the end line and have them shuffle along the end line to the left sideline. Always facing the opponent's court and the net, each player should shuffle three steps and simulate a passing motion and continue this throughout the entire drill. Once the players arrive at the left sideline they should shuffle forward two steps and shuffle to their right back to the right sideline. This movement pattern is continued until the players reach the center line, and then they go under the net, face the net, and shuffle from sideline to sideline, now using a two-step back-shuffle to work their way from the centerline all the way back to the end line. The player's movement throughout the drill resembles a winding snake, which is where we get the drill's name. The second progression of the drill have the players shuffle 3 steps and simulate a passing motion and shuffle 3 or more and pass continuing this action throughout the drill.

Continuous Passing

This drill is one that we use as a camp drill and also for a warm-up to stretching. It gets the players' heart rates to an acceptable level to stretch and helps the players with their skill development in the areas of forearm passing and overhead passing.

Have the players pick a partner; the two players must perform whatever the coach tells them to do. The players are to continuously pass the ball to each other without stopping as the coach changes what the players are doing. Here's an example of what you might have the players doing in this drill:

- Forearm-pass the ball to your partner using a low flat pass.
- Forearm-pass the ball to your partner using a very high pass.
- Forearm-pass the ball to yourself, then to your partner.
- Forearm-pass the ball to your self, and then side-pass the ball to your partner.
- Set the ball to your partner using a low flat set.
- Set the ball to your partner using a very high set.
- Set to yourself then set to your partner.
- Set to yourself, quarter turn and side-set to your partner.
- Set the ball to yourself, quarter turn, set to your self, quarter turn, set a back set to your partner.

After going through this progression your team will be more than warm enough to stretch!

Skills Relay

A great way to break up the normal routine that you might fall into is to run this drill. It is a great way to get the players warm enough to properly stretch. Split the team into two or three equal groups. Give a ball to each group and place them on one end line facing the opposite end line. Have the groups participate in a relay race that involves each player starting at the end line and going down and back. The next player in the group cannot receive the ball from her teammate until she passes the end line. The first group to finish wins! Here are some ideas for different types of races:

- Forearm-pass to self while walking forward.
- Forearm-pass to self while shuffling sideways.
- Set the ball to self while walking forward.
- Set the ball to self while shuffling sideways.
- Set the ball to self while using a crossover/grapevine step.
- Set the ball to self while skipping forward.
- Alternate forearm passing and setting the ball to themselves.

You can make the drill fun at the end by having the players bark like a dog or moo like a cow after each contact.

2

Passing Drills

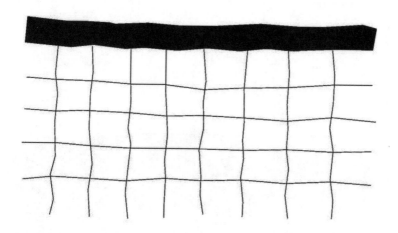

Key Phrases:

READY POSITION	MOVEMENT	CONTACT
Staggered stance	Shuffle	Thumbs together and down
Toes in-knees in	Centerline of body	Take ball between waist and knee level
Arms in front	Arms away	Drop your shoulder
Joints forward	Constant body height	Track the ball with eyes into the platform
Carry the tray		Drive legs and hips to the target

READY POSITION

MOVEMENT

CONTACT

Pipeline Passing Drill

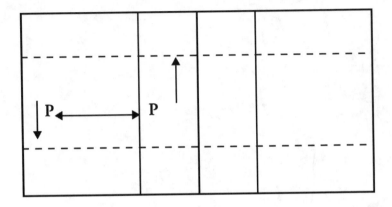

This drill is used to improve lateral movement and body positioning for forearm passing. Place two dotted lines on the court with floor tape about 12 feet apart. Both athletes start between the dotted lines and all passing occurs between the lines. Once the athlete closest to the net passes the ball to her partner, she shuffles to her right and touches the red line. She must shuffle back before the ball arrives from her partner. The partner is doing the same. After 15 passes by each player, have them shuffle to their left and back. Try starting at 10 reps each, then increase the number of reps with proficiency. This drill is a great conditioner for the legs and the core muscle group.

3-6-9

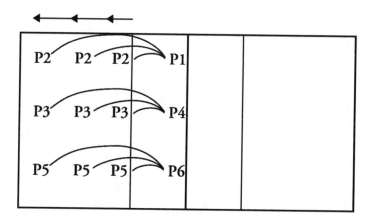

This drill is to help your players concentrate on their passing form, especially their platform. It also helps them to establish a uniformed height of their passes, which helps to run a more efficient offense.

Start with half your team at the net with balls in their hands and the other half at the three-meter line in a ready posture to pass. The coach will announce when all the people at the net should toss the balls at the same height to their partners. All the players at the three-meter line pass the ball to their partners in unison. The players at the net then pass the ball back to their partners at the three-meter line. After 10 successful passes are made in unison, the players at the three-meter line move back to an area between the three-meter line and the end line. After 10 successful passes are accomplished in unison at this distance, the players facing the net move to an area just inside the end line until the team is successful at this distance. This is a tough drill, but once your team is successful it's a huge confidence builder.

If the passes are out of unison, the coach should stop the drill and start over again. All 10 passes must be in unison before the next distance is attempted.

Butterfly Passing Series

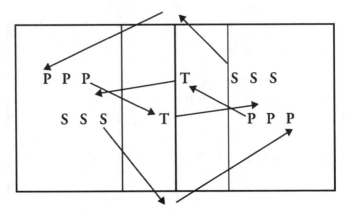

This is a drill that we used on a daily basis at ISU to warm up prior to stretching. It helps emphasize proper passing form and it gets the player's heart rate up to the level necessary to implement your stretching series.

Two separate groups can be run on the same court at the same time. Each group should have a passing line, a target line, and a serving/tossing line. Each player should stay within her original group of server/tosser-passer-target. The drill starts by the server/tosser throwing the ball over the net to the passer using a two-hand overhead toss. After tossing the ball, the server/tosser runs to her right around the net standard to the end of the passing line. The passer passes the ball to the target and follows the ball to the target line. The target catches the ball and runs to the server/tosser line. The target should be in the right front area, where your setter is normally located to run your offense, with her right hand up high as a target. Make sure the passer is calling the ball and that the target is yelling "here" so the passer has an audio target area. As the player's arms get warmer they can move back and proceed to a one-arm toss with her dominant arm.

The second progression of this drill series is to have the passer transition to her attack point outside the court after passing the ball. The goal for the passer is to arrive at the attack start point before the ball reaches the target. The target is working on getting to the ball quickly and catching the ball above her head with her body squared to set the ball to the outside. During this phase the server/tosser can toss the ball to herself and hits a roll shot to the passer.

The third progression involves the passer attacking the ball using a tip to the right front area of the opponent's court. The target is obviously setting the ball instead of catching it. The target should set the ball and then follow her set to cover the outside hitter. The server/tosser moves forward after contacting the ball to shag the ball that has been tipped by the passer/attacker and hands the ball to the target/setter, who goes to the server/tosser line.

The final progression of the drill starts with the server/tosser serving the ball from behind the end line to the opponent's left back. The passer/attacker passes the ball, transitions to her attack point, and then attacks the ball to zone 1 of the opponent's court with a three-quarter-speed line shot. Be sure that the target/setter covers the hitter after setting the ball. In progressions three and four you may want to only use your setters and right-side players to set the ball to the passer/attacker.

Merry-Go-Round

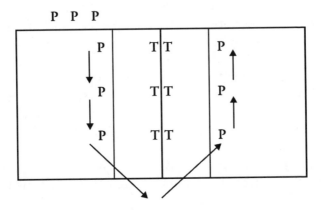

This is a great drill to emphasize the shuffle footwork that should be used in forearm passing and serve receive. Tossers/ targets stand at the net facing the court with balls in their hands prepared to underhand toss the balls just past the three-meter line to the passers. The passers start in a line outside the court, shuffle to their right into the court, and stop and pass a ball in front of each tosser/target back to the tosser/target. After passing the ball, the passer shuffles to the next tosser/ target, passes another ball, and proceeds to each tosser/tar-get around the net until all passers in that group have arrived in the right back area on the opposite side of the court. The passers then shuffle to their left and pass the balls to the toss-ers/targets until they return to the original starting spot. Once the first group of passers has completed the series, they switch places with the tossers/targets.

The second progression of the drill is to have the passers pass the ball from the area halfway between the three-meter line and the end line. This helps the passers work on the angle of their passing platform according to where they are in the court.

The last progression involves passers passing balls from the deep court near the end line. Throughout the progression of this drill be sure to emphasize that the players keep a constant height when shuffling or moving through the drill. Also make sure that that passers are stopping and "sticking" each pass.

This is a great drill to run when you have multiple courts in one gym, such as during camp.

Net Shuffle

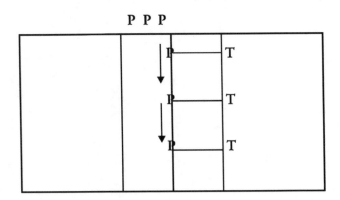

This drill utilizes the net as a training tool. Tossers are located behind the three-meter line and toss the ball toward the court's centerline. Passers start in the left front area on the opposite side of the net and shuffle along the centerline under the net in a low-posture passing stance and pass the ball to each of the tosser/targets. When all the passers in the first group get to the opposite side of the court, they shuffle back to their original starting location. Passers and tosser/targets then switch.

The next progression of the drill is to move the tossers to about six meters off the net to the area between the attack line and the end line. The passers also move forward and start the drill at the attack line. After the tosser slaps the volleyball, the passer shuffles backward until she is under the net while the tossers toss the ball for the passer to pass back to the tosser. This helps the passers to stay low with their shoulders forward while shuffling backward.

This drill helps the passers maintain a constant body posture while moving to pass. It is also a great conditioning drill for the legs and core muscle group.

Pass-n-Follow

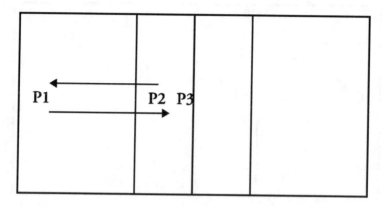

Divide your team up into groups of three. The drill starts with the volleyball in the hands of Passer 2 (P2). P2 starts the drill by tossing the ball to P1, who will pass the ball to P3. After P2 tosses the ball, she runs to her right and takes P1's place to receive the pass from P3. After P1 has passed the original tossed ball, she follows her pass to P3. The premise of the drill is to pass the ball and follow your pass by running to the right and creating a constant flow. The height of the pass will determine the difficulty of the drill. Start the drill with a relatively high pass and progress to a lower flatter pass, which will make the athletes run faster and control the ball better to be successful in the drill.

Self-Partner Series

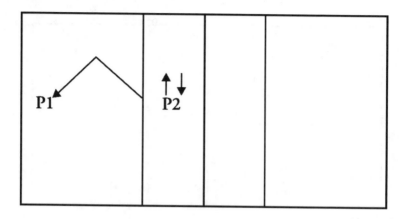

In this drill, players pair up with a partner and one ball. The drill is intended to help players work on adjusting their passing platform, depending on where they want to pass the ball, and promotes the use of their legs in their passing technique.

The first progression starts by P1 tossing the ball to P2, who forearm-passes the ball straight up to herself. She then adjusts her feet and passing platform to pass the ball in line with the centerline of her body to P1. P1 then passes the ball to herself, then to P2.

In the second progression, P1 tosses the ball to P2, who passes the ball to herself, turns so her left side is facing her partner, and then passes the ball off to her right side by moving her feet and angling her platform behind the ball toward P1. P1 repeats the process. Players should alternate passing the ball from their right side and left side.

The third progression involves the players working on alternating short flat passes with high passes. The short passes simulate free ball passes when you want to run a quicker offense and the higher passes are ones similar to those used to bump-set an outside hitter.

Be sure that the passers use their legs and have a flat platform on the high passes!

Pass-Harass

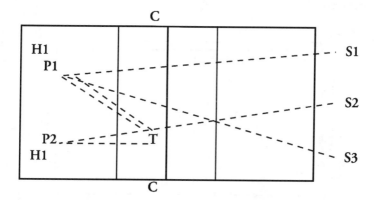

This drill involves having two passers (P1 and P2), two harassers (H1 and H2), a target setter (T), and three servers (S1, S2, and S3). The two harassers are to yell and talk to the passers trying to distract them from passing the ball to target. The harassers cannot make physical contact with the passers and must be sure that they don't get in the way of the passers as they move to pass the serve. You can place coaches or extra players in the left front and right front areas as targets for your setter to set to. After the passers successfully pass the desired number of balls to target, switch to new passers, harassers, and servers. The athletes love this drill, and it helps the passers focus on the ball and ignore distractions similar to what they might encounter from a hostile crowd.

Shuffle Series

Corner to Corner

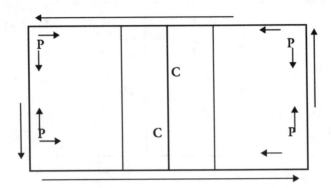

The first progression of the shuffle drill series is called "Corner to Corner." Start with three players at each corner of the court. The first player in each line moves to her left using three shuffle steps along her respective line and passes an imaginary ball to the right front. The player then shuffles back to the corner she started from and shuffles to the right three steps and passes again. From there, the player moves counterclockwise to the next corner and repeats the same progression. Once the player has arrived at the original starting spot the drill is complete. Be sure that all players run from corner to corner!

"W"

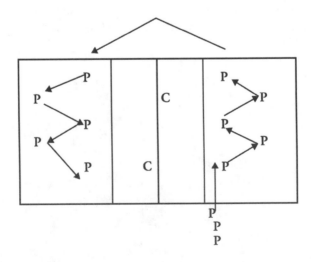

The second progression of the shuffle series is the "W." The players form a "W" with their movement patterns. The drill starts with your players outside the court at the three-meter line on the right side of the court. The drill starts by shuffling into the court and passing an imaginary ball to target in the left front area of the court, shuffling backward to the 5/6 seam and passing another imaginary ball, shuffling forward to the 3 zone for another pass, then back to the 1/6 seam to pass, and finally to the 2 zone for the last pass on that side of the court. The player then runs to the opposite side of the court and repeats the same "W" pattern on that side of the net.

Half Moon

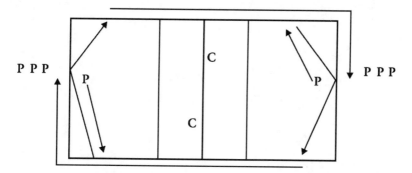

The last progression of the shuffle series is the "Half Moon" Drill. Split your team into two groups and have them line up off the court at the middle of the end line. A player steps into the court in the ready position and starts the drill by shuffling to the right in a half-moon/semicircle angle until she gets to the right sideline. At this point the player stops and simulates passing an imaginary ball to the right front. After passing, the player shuffles in a half-moon motion on the floor back past the middle of the end line and proceeds all the way to the left sideline and passes another ball. When the player passes the middle back area, the next player starts her shuffle. After passing one side the player runs to the opposite side of the net and performs the drill on the other side. The drill is complete when all players return to their original starting spot.

Once your players become proficient with their footwork patterns, try placing coaches in the right front areas where your setter normally stands and have the coaches toss balls to the passers in a random order; have the passers pass the ball back to the coaches.

Up and Back

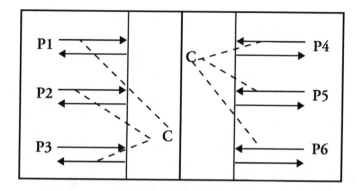

This drill helps your players work on their forward and backward shuffle movement. Be sure to emphasize that they keep their shoulders forward during movement so their platforms are out in front of their bodies. This drill also helps your players learn how to adjust their passing platforms depending on where they are in the court — whether it's deep in the court, close to the net, on the right side of the court, or on the left. Have the team perform the drill in groups of three. Each player should perform three sets of going forward from the end line to the attack line in each of the three backcourt areas, (right back, middle back, and left back). The coaches should be in the right front where the setter would be located and toss balls to the passers randomly.

Wall Work Progression

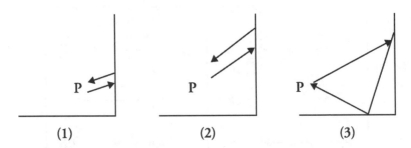

(1)   (2)   (3)

Diagram 1

The first progression of this drill involves the player stationing herself a short distance from the wall and passing the ball against the wall. The goal of this progression is to concentrate on the proper forearm passing stance and posture and having the athlete get a good feel for the ball coming off of her platform. The ball should be passed to a consistent spot on the wall that is about stomach-high. Try ten to fifteen reps in a row.

Diagram 2

The second progression involves the athlete moving about 3 or 4 feet farther back and passing the ball to a spot on the wall that is about head-high. The emphasis here is to move the feet to be sure the ball is in the centerline of the body and that the ball is being passed at a height off the floor between the athlete's knees and the waist.

Diagram 3

The third progression of this series has the athlete moving about 15 to 20 feet from the wall and passing to a designated spot on the wall after the ball has bounced off the floor once. I like this progression of the drill because the bounce off the floor can be unpredictable at times; it helps the passer work on quickness and adjustment skills.

Figure 8

Route of the passer-runner

Path of the ball:

1. ST2 tosses to P.
2. P passes ball to ST2.
3. ST2 passes ball to ST1.
4. ST1 passes ball to P.
5. P passes ball to ST1.
6. ST1 passes ball to ST2.
7. ST2 passes the ball to P.s

No, this isn't figure skating! This passing drill can also be used to work on the overhead pass. The drill involves three athletes. Two of the athletes are in stationary spots, and the third is the "passer/runner." The drill starts with ST2 tossing the ball to P, who forearm-passes the ball back to ST2. ST2 then passes the ball to ST1. P runs through the middle of the stationary players after passing the ball to ST2 and around ST2 and stops on the left side of ST2 to receive a pass from ST1 and passes the ball back to ST1. After passing the ball to ST1, P runs through the middle again, around ST1, and stops on the right side of ST1 to receive a pass from ST2. Once your passer/runner has passed 10 balls, switch positions so you have a new passer/runner.

This drill is a great conditioning drill that helps improve the foot speed of your passers and helps them with angling their platform to their target.

3

Serving Drills

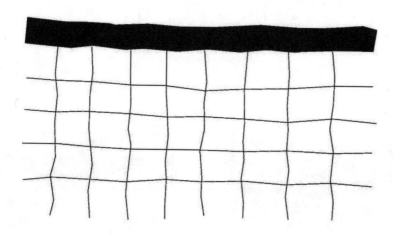

Key Phrases:

READY POSITION	MOVEMENT	CONTACT
Point front foot to target	Closed position	Stiff wrist
Form an "L" with the feet	Open position	Toss forward
Half step back with the right foot	Elbow check	Step and swing
Back foot at 45-degree angle	Hand check	
Knees flexed		

READY POSITION

MOVEMENT

CONTACT

Count on Me

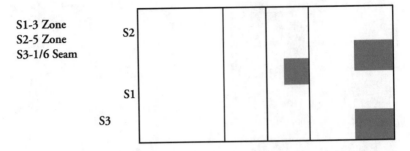

S1-3 Zone
S2-5 Zone
S3-1/6 Seam

Count on Me is a drill that you can use different times throughout your practices. Conduct the drill in the beginning, middle, and at the end of each practice. During each session, three different servers are selected who must hit specific service zone areas in the opponent's court. For every missed zone the entire team must run a set of sprints. This puts game-like pressure on the server to produce when the pressure is on. When first running this drill, have the players serve to spots they normally can hit. As the players become comfortable with the drill, give them serves that they usually struggle with to help them conquer their serving "demons." We will also give the last server a tougher serve and give the team the option to eliminate any sprints that they have accumulated if the last server hits her zone.

Space Invaders

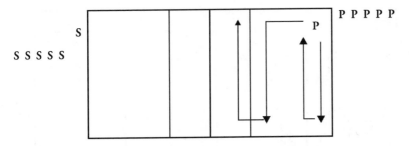

   While half your team is working on its serving technique, place the other half to work on shuffle passing footwork. The servers form a single file line behind the end line and serve balls in an attempt to hit the passers who are doing their shuffle footwork on the other side. The passers start in the right back area and shuffle across the back toward the left sideline. Once the passers reach the left sideline they shuffle forward one step and return back across the court toward the opposite sideline. The passers continue their shuffle footwork until they reach the net. If a passer is hit by a serve, she is out of the drill and must leave the floor. Once all of the passers reach the net the teams switch.

Player Target

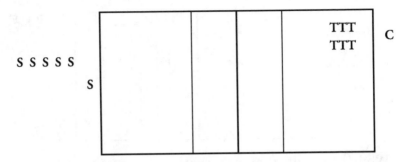

This is a fun way to work on zone serving, although at times it makes our athletic trainers nervous! Spilt your team into two groups—servers and targets. The targets lie on the floor in a service zone area. Each server serves a specific number of balls at the target zone. We usually have each server serve three balls. The servers score a point for every ball that hits the targets. Switch groups and see which team wins the round. We typically will do three zones at the beginning of practice and revisit the drill later in the practice for the other three service zones.

Stealth Serving

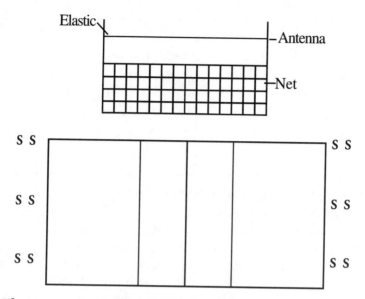

This is a great drill to help your players serve a hard, flat floater. The drill is called stealth serving because the servers must serve the ball between the net tape and a piece of waistband elastic that has been stretched from antenna to antenna. You want to alternate serves from one side to the other so you can determine which side accomplishes 10 serves under the radar of the elastic. Rotate your servers from the left, middle, and right areas along the end line so your players are comfortable and accurate in all three areas. This also provides you with three rounds for your team to compete against each other.

Hit the Coaches

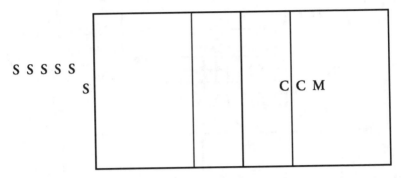

This drill is a variation of the "Player Target Drill," but gives the athletes a chance to hit the coaching staff with their serves. Don't be surprised if they get real excited about this!

The coaching staff lies in a specific service zone area and the players try to hit the staff with their serves. Split the team up into two groups and create a competition between the two groups. The group that hits the target the most wins. Similar to the "Player Target" drill, do three zones each at separate times during your practice. If you want to put some game-like pressure on your team, reduce the group's points for service errors.

Another variation on this drill is to make the athletes that miss the target lie on the floor next to the coaches until you only have one person left serving.

Serve the Seams

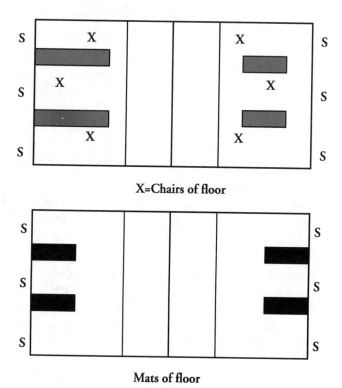

X=Chairs of floor

Mats of floor

The goal of this drill is to concentrate on serving the ball between the opponent's passers into the seams. You can run this drill in two ways. The first option is to place chairs on the floor and have your servers work on avoiding the chair by serving the ball in the seams between the chairs. The first side to serve 10 balls to the seam areas wins the drill. To make the drill more difficult you can place players in the chairs, and if the seated players can catch a serve, the serving team loses a point.

The second option in this drill is to place mats on the floor to provide actual targets for the servers.

Serve-n-Sprint

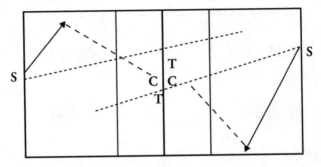

This drill is to help your athletes serve the ball and quickly get into the court to play defense, or pick up a setter dump. The server should serve the ball in the desired zone and then quickly run into the court to her defensive base position. Once the server arrives at the defensive position she must dig a ball from the coach. Have each server serve six balls and switch. The digger can work on picking up the dump from the setter simply by adding a setter on each side and having a coach toss to the setter. This way you are working on serving, transition, setter dump training, and defense against the dump all in one drill.

Serve, Sprint, and Dig

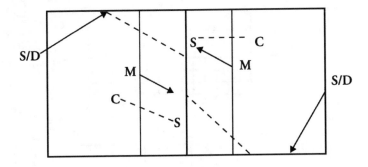

The next progression of the serve-n-sprint drill adds a middle hitter on each side along with setters. The coach moves behind the 3-meter line to toss the ball to the setter after the ball has been served, and the coach allows the appropriate time for the ball to arrive in the court before tossing the ball. The middle hitter runs a "1" attack and concentrates on hitting the ball to the left-back or right-back areas depending on which area the server goes to. The setter and middle are working on their timing for the first tempo attack; the server-defender is working on hitting the service zone, getting into the court and digging the quick attack.

Under-Over

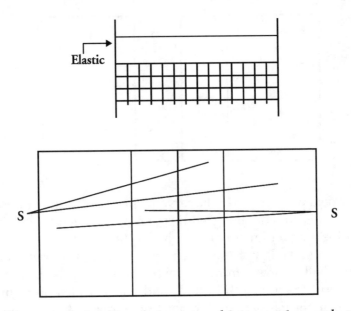

This is a good drill to help your athletes work on what we call the "yo-yo" serving strategy. It involves placing a piece of waistband elastic from one antenna to the other so there is a 2-foot opening between the net tape and the elastic. The object of the drill is to have your servers serve a deep zone floater that goes under the elastic followed by a short zone serve that drops just over the elastic. Once the server has accomplished both long- and short-serve combinations in the 1-2 zones, 3-6 zones, and 4-5 zones they are done.

4

Setting Drills

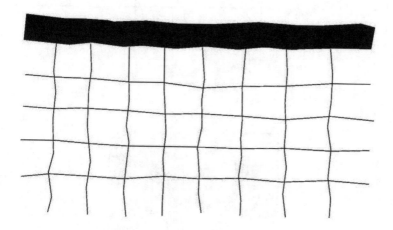

Key Phrases:

READY POSITION	MOVEMENT	CONTACT
Feet shoulder-width apart	Hands up early	Pads on ball
Five steps to proper hand	Hands up high	Flow with hands and arms
Two liter chug hands	Get behind the ball	Follow set and cover the hitter
Ball-shaped hands	Square to target	
Knees flexed		
Right food forward		

READY POSITION

MOVEMENT

CONTACT

Set-n-Follow

This drill is designed to help your setters with their speed, footwork, and squaring up to their target. Divide your team into groups of three, each group with one ball. The drill starts with B having the ball and tossing it underhand to A, who will set the ball to C. After B tosses the ball, she follows the ball by running to her right and replacing A. By the time B arrives at her spot, C is receiving the ball from A and has set the ball to B. The basic premise of the drill is to set the ball and follow it to the spot you just set it to.   Make sure that your athletes get to their spot before the ball arrives, square to target and follow through with their window to the target. This drill can also help in following the set to cover the hitter.

Figure Eight

Similar to the Forearm Passing Figure 8 drill, this is a great drill for beginners and advanced players alike. The drill helps with the aspects of body positioning, quickness, and skill development of the overhead pass or set. The drill involves three players, one runner, and two stationary people. The runner starts the drill to the right of ST1 and receives a tossed ball from ST2 and sets the ball back to ST2. Immediately after setting the ball, the setter-runner cuts across the middle and around ST2 to the left side of ST2 and waits for a set from ST1, who had received a set from ST2. After setting the ball from ST1 back to ST1, the setter-runner cuts across the middle and around ST1 to receive a set coming from ST2. After the setter-runner has set 10 balls, switch positions.

Wall Work Progression

This is something that we did with our setters on a daily basis. The drill series helps to make sure that the setters are using the correct hand positioning for their window and that they are taking the ball correctly in relationship to their body. Your athletes need to find a clear spot on the wall that will allow them to set the ball about 30 to 40 feet high without hitting an obstruction.

Close to wall: The athlete positions herself only a few inches from the wall with her right foot slightly forward and knees flexed. The ball should be in the setter's hands, which are in the proper window position. The setter will set the ball against the wall quickly, working on keeping the window in its proper position and keeping her arms up high so they are making contact at their hairline or higher. The setter should accomplish 100 contacts before moving to the next progression.

3 feet off: The athlete now moves about 3 feet away from the wall to set 50 balls to a designated spot on the wall. It might help to put some tape on the wall in the shape of a box to act as the target. The setter sets balls to the target on the wall continuously until her 50 contacts are accomplished. The things to emphasize here are to move the feet quickly, keep the hands high, make sure they have "ball-shaped hands," and to work on the transfer of weight from the back foot to the front as they are setting the ball. The drill also helps your setters with "squaring to target."

Set and bounce: The last progression in this series helps the setter move her feet, adjust the lower body to various height sets, and improves reflexes. The setter moves a few more feet away from the wall and sets the ball to a spot on the wall about 30 feet from the floor. After the ball is set to the wall, the setter allows the ball to bounce once and then sets the ball to the spot on the wall and repeats the process until she has accomplished 50 sets.

Walking Progression

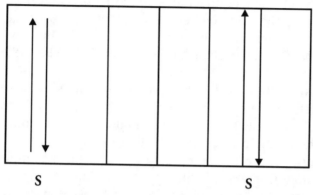

S   S

The walking progression is also something that our setters did on a daily basis. It helps them get their "window" established and also helps with their footwork and foot speed.

This progression also is a great way to improve your players' abilities to perform multiple tasks at once. This series also puts your setter into all the possible body positions that they will experience in playing the game.

All of the progressions with the exception of the Up and Down section involve the setter moving from one sideline to the other and back again. Start the players on the right sideline, and have them perform each progression to the left sideline and then back to the right sideline.

Set forward to self: The setter simply sets the ball forward to herself as she walks from one sideline and back. Be sure that the setter is calling "mine" before every contact to develop good communication habits. The setter should walk a straight line and keep her hands high at all times. Be sure that the setter is using the same technique that she would if she was setting a first tempo ball, aka "1" ball.

Set backward to self: The setter performs the same progression as above but this time she is walking backward while setting the ball to herself. All the setter has to do is rotate her window/palms up towards the ceiling more and follow through slightly backward. The technique used here would be that of setting a "6," or back first tempo ball.

Shuffle footwork: Next, the setter turns and faces the net and side sets the ball to herself as she shuffles to her left. The setter will be able to direct the ball in the direction she is moving by slightly dropping her left shoulder lower than the right. Once the setter has gone from sideline to sideline and back, she should turn herself around so her back is to the net; repeat the footwork.

Crossover footwork: Also known as grapevine or carioca, the setter uses a crossover step while facing the net and then, when done, switches to face the end line. The setter must compensate for the further distance that she will cover with this footwork pattern by setting the ball off to the side more.

Skipping forward: We like to use the skipping technique to help our setters make emergency-type sets that are well off the net. In this progression, the setter sets the ball forward as she is using a high-knees skip.

Skipping backward: The last progression of this series involves the setter skipping backward while back-setting the ball.

B-Ball Goal-Three Point Line

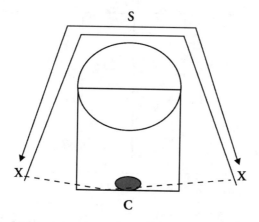

The Basketball Goal drill is a great way to help your setters improve their footwork, foot speed, and perfect the ability to "square to target" before setting the ball. The setter starts the drill at the top of the key outside the 3-point line. The coach stands under the basketball goal and starts the drill by slapping the ball. The setter runs to her right outside the 3-point line to the area where the coach has tossed a ball. The setter must get to the spot, get her body squared to target, and set the ball to the basketball goal. Once the ball has been set, the setter releases and runs outside the 3-point line to the left side of the court and receives another ball from the coach. Each setter should set 5 balls from the left and 5 balls from the right before switching to another setter. The coach can make the drill as easy or as difficult as desired by varying the height of the toss.

Weighted Ball Progression

					S1
				S1	
			S1		
		S1			
	S1				
S1					
S1					
S2	S2	S2	S2	S2	S2
A	B	C	D	E	F

At Indiana State we use a basketball, a volleyball, and the Baden VXT4 Heavy Setter weighted ball for this drill. Make sure to train both your setters and right-side athletes with this drill. Obviously you want your setters to have a strong upper body to handle their high demand throughout a match, but you also must remember that your right-side athletes will set their share of balls throughout the season and typically they will set a high ball to the outside. This drill enables them to develop their upper-body strength so they can easily, and accurately, set the ball across the court.

Start the drill with two athletes standing about a foot apart, facing each other. The order of which ball you use is basketball, then heavy setter ball, and then the volleyball. First go through the following progression with the setters standing on the floor, then go through the progression again with the setters performing jump sets.

A - 1 foot apart-10 touches each with basketball, heavy ball, then volleyball

B - 3 feet apart-10 touches each with basketball, heavy ball, then volleyball

C - 6 feet apart-10 touches each with basketball, heavy ball, then volleyball

D - 12 feet apart-10 touches each with the basketball, heavy ball, then volleyball

E - 15 feet apart-volleyball only
F - 30 feet apart-volleyball only

Box Target Series

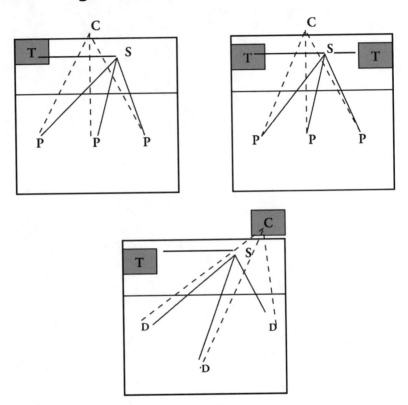

The purpose of this drill series is to work on your setter's placement proficiency. It is easier for the setters to set a ball to a stationary, visible target to get a feel for how to set particular sets. The drill involves having a person stand on a coaching box, or chair, in the zone that the set should be set. The target on the box should have her hands held up at the same height that an attacker would be when attacking that particular set. I suggest having each of your setters set 10 balls in a row in each progression before switching. This will help them get into a flow, or groove, so they realize how they should be setting that particular set. I like to have my setters set balls that are coming from a pass to simulate a game-like scenario. The coach just throws balls over to the passers from the opposite court. Be sure that your setters are always jump-setting when possible. The progression is as follows:

A - Set "5" to left front

B - Set "4" to left front

C - Set "9" to right front

D - Set "8" to right front

E - Set "2" to middle

F - Set "7" to right front

G - Set "3" to left front

H - Set "1" to middle

I - Set "6" to right front

J - Set to "4" or "5" to left front or "8" or "9" to the right front

K - Set "3" to left front or "8" to right front

Hit the Zones-Setter Dump

		2	1
P			
P	S	3	6
P		4	5

This drill is designed to help your setters and right sides work on hitting all six zones in the opponent's court using a variety of techniques. It is important for your setters and right sides to be able to perform all the dumping options depending on what comes available. You can perform this drill from a coach's toss; however, I suggest using a couple of your primary passers in the drill if possible. You might as well make the drill as game-like as possible. Follow the progression below:

A - Dump to zone 1 with right hand

B - Dump to zone 2 with right hand

C - Dump to zone 3 with right hand

D - Dump to zone 4 with right hand

E - Dump to zone 1 with left hand

F - Dump to zone 2 with left hand

G - Dump to zone 3 with left hand

H - Dump to zone 4 with left hand

I - Dump to zone 1 with both hands

J - Dump to zone 2 with both hands

K - Dump to zone 3 with both hands

L - Dump to zone 4 with both hands

M - Dump to zone 5 with both hands

N - Dump to zone 6 with both hands

Floating Blockers Challenge

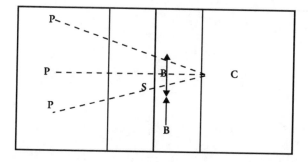

This drill is used to help the setters and right side players recognize when and where to dump the ball over the net and how to perform a variety of attacks with both hands. This drill was created to put the setter or right side player in every game situation that they might encounter. Put two blockers on the opposite side of the net along with the coach. The coach punches balls over the net to the primary passers, who will pass balls to the setter. Tell the blockers in the middle and left front to vary where they line up as the ball is coming into the setter so the setter must read the blockers to determine what dump option would be the best under those circumstances. The more your setters perform this drill, the better they will be in recognizing situations come game time. Once a setter or right-side player has scored on 10 dumps, switch personnel.

You can modify the drill by making it a competition between the setters and the blockers. The first group to score 10 points wins.

5

Blocking Drills

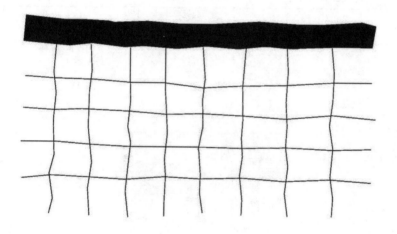

Key Phrases:

READY POSITION	MOVEMENT	CONTACT
Loaded legs	Lead with the hands	Penetrate early
"L" with the arms (forearms parallel to the net, upper arms parallel to the floor)	Glide over the floor	Press the palms
"W" with hands	Tight to the net	Turn hands to 3/6
Ball-shaped hands	Close the block	Tighten from tips to toes
Knees flexed	Seal the net	
Right foot forward		

READY POSITION

MOVEMENT

CONTACT

Traffic Cop Blocking Drill

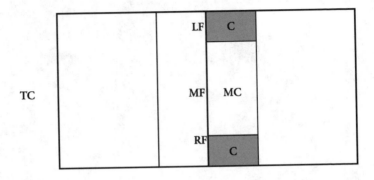

This is one of the best conditioning drills for your middle blockers. Running them from "pin to pin" (antenna to antenna) is the best way to work on their endurance, technique, and footwork. Start with a left side blocker (LF), a middle blocker (MF), and a right side blocker (RF) in their base defense positions in their loaded blocking stance. On the opposite side of the net are two coaches, or players, on boxes or chairs with balls in their hands. A third coach or player is in the middle, but is not on a chair since we want him/her to be mobile and able to attack in a number of areas along the net.

The last person we need, which is the most important, is the traffic cop! The traffic cop (TC), is located behind the end line on the same side of the net as the blockers and will signal to the attackers as to who will attack the next ball. Once the attacker receives the signal from the traffic cop, she slaps her volleyball, which provides the blockers with the information they need to key on the attacker. The blockers then defend the attacker, and after that quickly return to their base defensive positions. The drill continues at this quick pace until the blockers stop a predetermined number of balls. Be sure that the attackers don't just hit balls at the block! Keep the off-blockers honest, and make sure they are in position for the off-speed shot.

Block Pickup

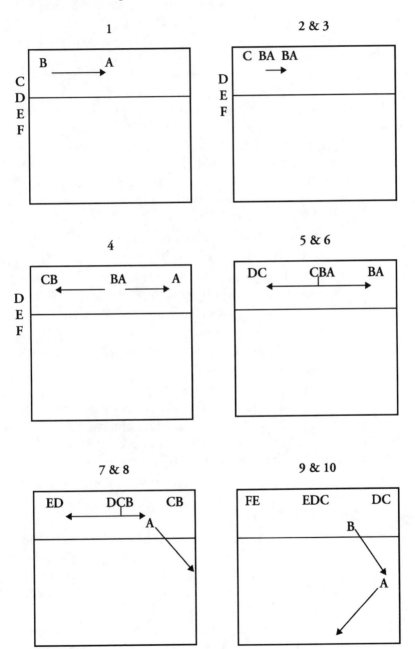

1

2 & 3

4

5 & 6

7 & 8

9 & 10

This is a great drill for working on all aspects of blocking in a game-like setting. It helps your athletes with their loaded stance, footwork, technique, communication, penetration, and even their backcourt movement skills. Below you will find the progression and diagrams for this drill. If you want to add a more game-like component to the drill, try having your coaching staff on the opposite side of the net on boxes hitting balls at the block to insure that they are closing, sealing, and penetrating. Be careful of balls rolling under the net though!

1. "A" starts the drill in the left front in a loaded block stance and performs a solo block. She then uses a step-cross-hop pattern to the middle of the net and solo blocks there. While "A" is blocking in the middle, "B" is blocking on the left side.

2. "A" then uses the step-cross-hop footwork to her left to close to "B" and they both block on the left side.

3. "A" and "B" then move to the middle together, while "C" steps up to the left front. While "A" and "B" block in the middle, "C" is blocking on the left side.

4. "A" then moves to her right to block solo on the right side while "B" moves back toward the left side to block with "C" on the left side.

5. "A" then uses the step-cross-hop footwork to return to the middle to participate in a triple block in the middle with "B" and "C." While the triple block is being performed in the middle, "D" has stepped into the drill in the left front and is performing a solo block.

6. "C" now goes back to the left front to block with, and to pick up "D", while "B" and "A" move to the right front to block together.

7. In this progression, "A" transitions off the net after the block with "B" and simulates setting a ball to the left front while "B" transitions to the middle to put up a triple block with "C" and "D," and "E" is performing a solo block in the left front.

8. "D" now goes to her left to the left front to block with and pick up "E" while "C" and "B" transition to the

right front to block to-gether. "A" has now transitioned to the right back area of the court using shuffle footwork to simulate digging a ball.

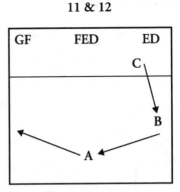

11 & 12

9. "A" continues using her shuffle footwork to move to the middle back area to dig another ball while "B" is setting a ball to the left side attacker after transitioning off the net after her block and "C" has transitioned to the middle to put up the triple block with "D" and "E," and "F" has stepped up to the net in the left front to solo block.

10. "D" and "C" spilt from "E" and transition to the right front to block while "E" is transitioning to the left front to block with "F," and "A" and "B" are performing their defensive movement in the backcourt in the left back and right back, respectively.

11. "F" now transitions to the middle to triple block with "E" and "D," and "G" steps into the drill and solo blocks in the left front. "B" and "C" continue their movement in the backcourt.

12. The drills flow continues with "F" moving to the left front to block with "G" and "E," and "D" moving to the right front to block.

The drill continues until "G" has arrived in the left back area. We usually go through the drill twice at a time, so "A" would simply get back in line and be "picked up" by "G" so the drill has continuous flow until "F" arrives in the left back for the second time.

Overpass

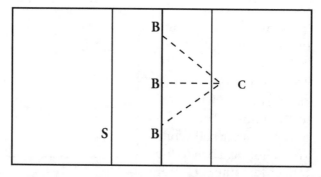

The easiest way to get a point other than an ace is an over-pass kill or block by one of your blockers. These are opportunities that you hate to see wasted, so spend some time on this simply drill. Place your three blockers at the net in the positions that they typically play. The coach will toss balls over the net in random order and at different trajectories at the blockers. The blockers must decide whether to go up and attack the ball, block the ball, or pull off the net and set a free ball to the setter. Balls that come over the net or at the net with a high trajectory usually should be attacked using a spike swing, while balls that have a lower, flatter trajectory should be blocked back into the opponent's court. Make sure that the blockers aren't just swinging or blocking without a purpose! Your blockers should be directing the ball to areas of the court that are usually open in an overpass situation. Be sure that you toss a ball over periodically that will force the blockers to pull off the net and pass it to the setter. All three blockers should transition off the net in this circumstance so they are available to run a free ball play set. Once each player in the group of three has converted five balls, get three more blockers into the drill.

Blind Blocking

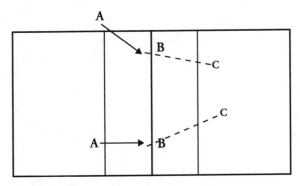

   This is one of the best drills I use for helping my athletes "front the attacker." The most common problem with inexperienced blockers is that they watch the ball too much and don't key on the attacker's movement and angle of approach. In this drill, the blocker can't see the ball until the last moment since the coach is tossing the ball over the net from behind the blocker. Position the attackers on the left side of the court in a position so they can make a full approach to attack the ball that is tossed by the coach. The blockers are placed in their normal start blocking stance and location. The blocker simply watches the attacker and determines their angle of approach and makes the necessary adjustment along the net to front the attacker. Once a blocker has blocked five balls, replace the blocker.

Block Merry-Go-Round

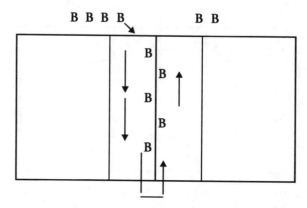

Although there are three progressions to this drill, all three use the same flow pattern. All blockers start in a single-file line at the left front area on the left side of the net. Once the blocker performs the required blocking footwork, she moves along the net to her right, goes around the net to the right side of the net, and then continues her footwork pattern to her right until she gets to the right sideline. At that point, the blockers that have completed the drill wait for the rest of the group. Once everyone has arrived at the right sideline on the right side of the court they perform the drill to their left until they arrive at the original starting point.

Hop: In this blocking footwork pattern the blocker merely makes a shuffle step to her right into a loaded block position and jumps off the floor to block over the net into the opponent's court. This blocking footwork is used by middle blockers to make quick adjustments when trying to stop first-tempo balls by the opponent and by outside hitters to make adjustments to front hitters.

Cross-Hop: The Cross-Hop footwork involves making the first step with the far foot by crossing over the body toward the desired direction of movement, followed by a hop step with the other foot. The Cross-Hop footwork covers more ground than the Hop footwork. It is usually used by outside hitters that want to assist in blocking in the middle or by the middle hitter to help block balls that are not set to far outside or to the right side attackers.

Step-Cross-Hop: The Step-Cross-Hop footwork starts with a small step with the foot closest to the direction the blocker wants to move, followed by a crossover step with the other foot, and finally a hop step to close the block. The blocking footwork pattern that covers the most ground is the Step-Cross-Hop footwork. It is typically used by the middle blockers to close to the right and left in defending outside attacks by the opponent.

Transition Footwork Pattern — Middle Attacker

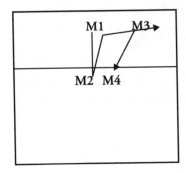 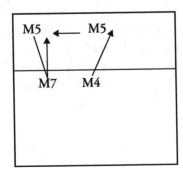

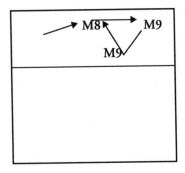

We emphasize footwork patterns on a daily basis. The athletes must become so comfortable with these patterns that they can react to a situation and perform the footwork without thinking about it. It is very similar to training in the martial arts. Do so many repetitions that it becomes a reaction to a situation.

Here is the progression for the middle hitter/blocker:

A - The middle hitter starts the drill in her base defense position at the net. (M1)

B - The middle takes a hop step to the left and blocks.

C - The middle then transitions off the net behind the 3-meter line. (M2)

D - The middle then makes a slide approach to hit an "8."

E - After the slide attack, the middle blocks in the right front area. (M3)

F - From there the middle transitions to her spot behind the 3-meter line and goes in for a "1" attack. (M4)

G - After the "1" attack, the middle returns to her base defense position. (M5)

H - The middle then uses a step-cross-hop footwork pattern to block on the left side against the opponent's right side attacker. (M6)

I - After coming down from the block, the middle transitions behind the 3-meter line and then goes in for a "3" attack. (M7)

You can vary the types of attacks and blocks as desired.

Transition Footwork Pattern — Left Side Attacker

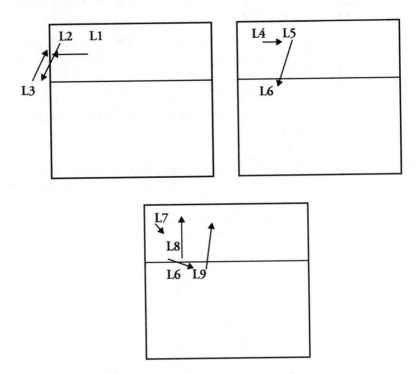

Transition footwork pattern for the left side attacker simulates the different blocking and attacking scenarios that they will encounter in a game. Here is the progression for this drill:

A - The left side starts the drill in her base defense position with her legs loaded. (L1)

B - The left side uses a hop step to the outside to block a right side attack. (L2)

C - From there, the left side transitions outside the court and then goes in to attack a "5" set. (L3)

D - After attacking, the left side moves back into her base defensive position. (L4)

E - From here she uses the cross-hop footwork pattern to help block a middle attack. (L5)

F - After landing, the left side transitions off the net behind the 3-meter line and goes in for a "32" attack. (L6)

G - After the attack, the left side returns to her base defense position. (L7)

H - From here she transitions off the net to play defense in the left front area and plays up an off-speed shot from the opponent. (L8)

I - After digging the ball, the left side transitions behind the 3-meter line and goes in for a "2" attack. (L9)

Transition Footwork Pattern — Right Side Attacker

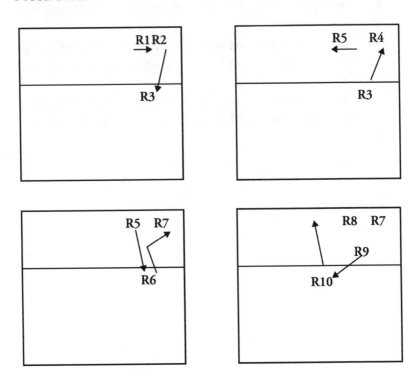

The right side attacker-blocker has a few additional components that the middle and left side attacker-blockers do not. You should add the necessary components to make this drill game-like for your right side players. Here is the progression:

    A - Start with the right side player in her base defense position. (R1)

    B - Have the right side use a hop step to the outside to front and block a left side attacker. (R2)

    C - From here the right side transitions off the net, behind the 3-meter line, and goes in for a "9" attack. (R3)

    D - After the attack, the right side returns to her base defense position. (R4)

    E - From here, the right side uses a cross-hop footwork pattern to help block in the middle. (R5)

F - After coming down from the block, the right side transitions off the net behind the 3-meter line and then goes in for a slide attack on an "8" ball. (R6)

G - After the attack, the right side moves into her base defense position. (R7)

H - From there the right side uses a hop step to her left to block a "3" ball by the opponent. After the block the right side turns off the net and sets a ball to the left side attacker. (R8)

I - After the set the right side returns to her base defense position at the net and then turns off the net and moves to the right front area to defend an off-speed shot by the opponent's right side attacker. (R9)

J - After digging the ball, the right side transitions behind the 3-meter line and then goes in for a "2" attack. (R10)

Transition Footwork Pattern — Setter

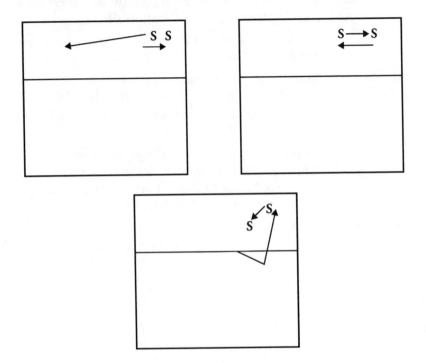

The setter's footwork patterns are similar to the right side's patterns, except, of course, that she is setting the ball in transition as opposed to transitioning off the net to attack. Here's a footwork patterns to use for your setter:

A - Start with the setter at the net and using a hop footwork pattern to block line. After the block the setter should open into the court, locate the ball, and go through the proper footwork to set a ball to the left side attacker, which includes covering the hitter.

B - The setter should then get back to her base defense position at the net and use the cross-hop footwork to help block a middle attack. After the block the setter should transition to the right front area to receive the dig and set an "8" back to the middle, then cover.

C - After covering, the setter should return to her base defense position at the net and then make a hop step to the inside or her left to block the opponent's attempt to run a "3."

D - After coming down from the block, the setter sets a middle ball and drops to cover.

E - The setter returns to her base defense position and from here pulls off the net to play defense in the right front looking for an off-speed shot from the opponent's right side player.

F - After digging the ball, the setter transitions from her defensive position to behind the 3-meter line to attack a "9" that is set by the right back.

G - After attacking the ball the setter returns to her base defense position, then opens into her court as if the opponent sent over a free ball, jumps to set and then dumps into the opponent's court.

6

Individual Defense Drills

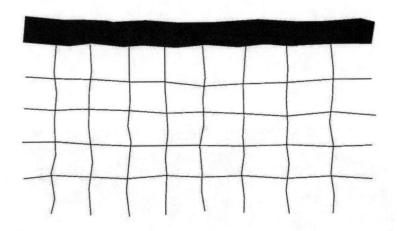

Key Phrases:

READY POSITION	MOVEMENT	CONTACT
Wide staggered base	Keep chest to floor	Arms away
Toes and knees in	Pre-hop	Drop shoulder
Joints up – joints forward	Read the attacker	Angle platform
Chest to floor	Arms in front	Track with eyes
		Absorb the impact

READY POSITION

MOVEMENT

CONTACT

Pivot and Dig

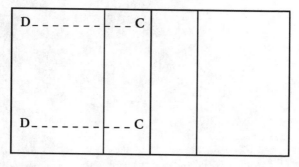

This is a drill that will help your athletes improve their reaction time when playing defense. Place your diggers in the backcourt with the coaches at the net. The defensive players should be in their defensive ready position, but should have their backs to the net. The coach will slap the ball, which is the player's cue to turn around, locate the ball, and dig it back to the coach. Once the player has dug 10 balls to target, she is done. The coach can control the pace of the drill by how much time he allows from the slap of the ball until he attacks it and the speed of the attack.

Middle Back Cone Drill

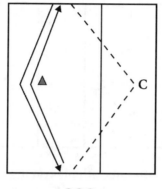

P P P

This is a good conditioning drill that helps to get the team in a defensive state of mind. Place a rubber cone in the middle back area about 3 feet into the court. It is best to have about 3 to 4 players going through the drill at a time; that way they get maximum contacts in a short period of time. Start with the players in the right back area. They step into the court and dig a ball coming from the coach. After digging the ball, the player runs from her position around the cone to the left back area and digs another ball from the coach. Once that player has dug a second ball, she steps off the court and waits for the other players to execute the drill. The drill is repeated going back the other way. Have the group go through this progression three times before putting a new group on the floor.

Prone Passing

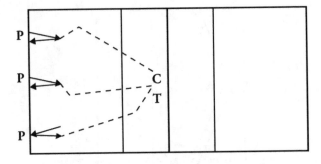

This drill begins with three athletes on the floor on their stomachs at the end line facing the net. The coach is situated at the net in the middle front. When the coach slaps the volleyball, the athlete in the right back area must push up off the floor and use a run-through technique to get to the ball and play it to target. The coach should use a bounce pass to make sure the ball is low enough to keep the player in a low movement stance. After playing the ball, the athlete immediately runs back to her original position on the floor. The coach proceeds to slap another ball, which is the signal to the person on the floor in the middle back to perform the same act. The drill continues until the group of three has accomplished a set number of balls to the target.

If you want to make the drill more game-like, try having the players on the floor outside the court near their base defense positions. In doing this the players learn how to run down a ball from their defensive positions and can work on the platform in passing those balls.

Cover-the-Court Defense Drill

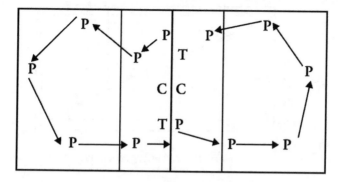

In this drill, one defender covers the entire floor in a trip around the perimeter of the court. The coach should locate him/herself in the middle front on the left side of the court for the first half of the drill and will simply switch to the opposite side of the net for the second half. The drill starts by having the player start in the left front area at the net in a block stance. The player will transition off the net and play up a tip from the coach. After playing up the ball the player transitions to the left back area to dig a ball from the coach. After digging the ball in the left back area the player transitions to the middle back area and digs another ball. From here the player transitions to the right back area and digs another ball. The player transitions to the right front area to pick up a tip from the coach. The player is now halfway through the drill as she steps under the net and assumes a block stance as the coach also moves to the other side of the court. After the coach slaps the ball, the player transitions off the net to dig a ball behind the attack line. The player then transitions to the deep left back corner and digs another ball. From there the player moves to the middle back and digs another ball. The last two contacts for the player are when she transitions to the right back area and digs a ball and then picks up a tip from the coach in the right front area

Butterfly Run Thru

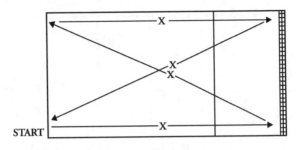

X – INDICATES PLAYING A BALL

This is a great drill to get the team going! It can bring out that tough defensive state of mind that you are always looking for in a team. Start by splitting the team up into two groups, but I wouldn't have more than six players going through the drill at once. It is important that the shaggers do a great job of keeping balls off the court in this drill since there is quite a bit of movement by the people in the drill.

Start with a group in the right back corner of the court and have them perform run-through passes while going down the right sideline. From there they run from the right front corner to the left back corner, playing a ball around midcourt. From the left back corner they proceed down the left sideline while playing up balls just past the 3-meter line. From there the players go from the left front to the right back corner.

Make sure that the players are moving in a low posture and that they concentrate on having their platform angled to the target and stay behind the ball.

Stay Alive!

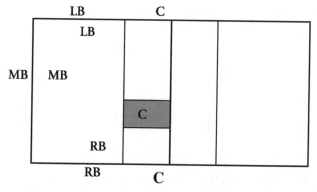

This is one of the favorites of just about every team I've coached. It is a competitive drill that pits the coach against the defenders. Before starting the drill, it is necessary to tape off a box in the right front area of the court. Make the box a size that represents an area in which your setter normally would be receiving the ball from your passers or defenders. Three defenders at a time attempt to keep the ball alive as long as possible. We keep track as to the number of digs a group receives. If the ball hits the floor, those three are out, and three more replace them. The drill starts when someone tosses a ball to the coach in the box, who attacks the ball at the defenders. If the ball is dug to the coach in the box, the coach continues to attack the ball at the defenders. If the first ball contacted by the defenders doesn't go to the box, the defenders can set the ball to the coaches standing in the left front or right front, who will attack the ball. These digs also count toward the group's total. Keep track of the highest number of digs in this drill so your team can try to break the record the next time you run the drill. Obviously, the coach in the box can make this drill as easy or difficult as he wants.

Double-Dig Defense Drill

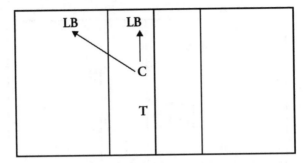

This drill was developed to help our defenders keep their weight forward when they are in their defensive stance and to be able to pick up off-speed shots and balls off the block. You will want to run this drill from every possible scenario that your team will encounter, such as attacks from the right side, left side, and in the middle. To describe the drill we will use the scenario of the left back defending an attack out of the middle.

Have the coach in the middle front on the same side of the net as the defender. Place a target in the right front area for the left back player to dig to. The left back player should start the drill in her overpass-dump position, and when the coach slaps that ball she transitions to her base defense position. The coach then attacks a hard-driven spike at the defender, who digs the ball to target. Immediately after the player digs the first ball, the coach tips a ball into the court and the player must explode out of her digging stance and run down the second ball to play it to target. Make sure you cover all of the following scenarios:

A - Left back digs attack from opponent's right front.

B - Left back digs attack from opponent's middle front.

C - Left back digs attack from opponent's left front.

D - Middle back digs attack from opponent's right front

E - Middle back digs attack from opponent's middle front.

F - Middle back digs attack from opponent's left front.

G - Right back digs attack from opponent's right front

H - Right back digs attack from opponent's middle front

I - Right back digs attack from opponent's left front.

7

Attack Drills

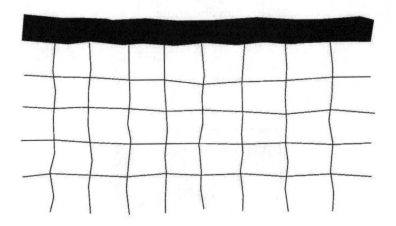

Key Phrases:

READY POSITION	MOVEMENT	CONTACT
Mid-range stance	Three step approach	High in front of shoulder
Weight forward	Quick and explosive	Body behind the ball
	Accelerate	Big Hand at contact
	Left/right/left – right hand	Snap the wrist
	High Bow and arrow	

READY POSITION

MOVEMENT

CONTACT

Hourglass Attack Drill

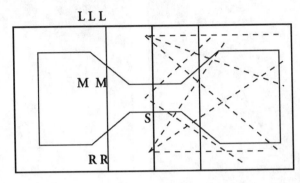

Although most defensive systems are considered perimeter defenses, most teams don't play their defense on the perimeter. Most players tend to suck into the court and leave the outside of the court open. Another factor to consider is that blocking at the collegiate and club levels force hitters to hit around the block, but still keep it in the court.

In this drill we tape off the court in an hourglass shape to provide the teams with a visual target to attack. The first progression of the drill is to simply put a setter on one side and have the attackers attempt to hit the target area. To make the drill competitive, separate the team into two squads and see which squad can accomplish 15 kills in the outer zone first. You could also have the positions compete against each other (middles, outsides, right sides).

15 in a Row Attack Drill

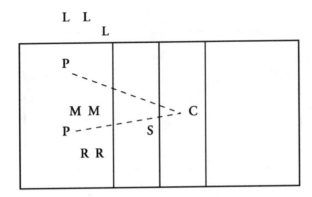

We have found that this is a great drill to help our attackers to reach high and get full extension on their arm swing. It also helps our attackers to hit the deep third of the opponent's court. The goal of the drill is to have your attackers successfully attack 15 balls in a row into the opponent's court without a hitting error or having the ball hit the net tape. Use your defensive specialists to act as primary passers, which puts pressure on them to get the ball accurately to target. Place the coach on the opposite side of the net to toss the balls over to the passers.

The drill can be modified to make it harder by taping off high-scoring sections of the opponent's court and only counting shots to those areas toward the 15 in a row. If you do this, I suggest starting off at 5 or 10 in a row and working up top 15 in a row.

Count on Me Attack Drills

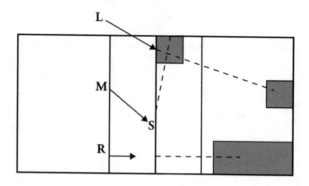

A great way to simulate the pressure that the players might experience in the game is to have them do this drill. Predetermine players to participate in the drill, and run the drill several times throughout your practice. Each time you run the drill use three players to attack particular shots that they have to accomplish or the team has to run a set of down-n-back sprints. The second best pressure than game pressure is peer pressure! In the diagram above, we have the left side attacker hitting a deep shot to zone 6 of the opponent's court, the middle tipping a shot to zone 2 and the right side attacker hitting a deep line shot to the corner. We will allow the team to accept a double or nothing bet if we get to the third attacker and the first two have missed. This puts more pressure on the third attacker, but also can make them a real hero with the team if she scores!

Tool Time

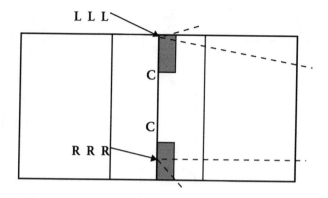

This drill is meant to improve your players' ability to handle balls that are set a little tight to the net and give them an option other than just trying to force the ball through the block. Place two boxes at the net on the side opposite of the attackers with blockers on each box. You can have the right side and left side attackers performing the drill at the same time. A coach, or another athlete, will be tossing balls to the respective position attackers. Have your tossers toss the ball in various locations on and off the net, but the majority of balls should be tossed tight. The attackers approach the ball and attempt to "tool," or deflect the ball off the hands of the blockers out of bounds. We use two techniques when running this drill. The first is the "wipe off," where we try to hit the ball out of bounds toward the outside of the court and the other is a high hard shot off the blocker's hands that catches the fingertips and sails deep out of bounds. Once each group of three attackers has been successful in scoring with 10 tool shots, switch hitters. I suggest eventually using a setter to set the balls so it is a more game-like situation for the attackers.

Be sure to work on using a tipping action when tooling the block. Sometimes, a simple redirection of the ball with a tip off the block will score an easy point. The key to using the "tool tip" is to make sure the attacker's hand is behind the ball and pushes slightly into the hands of the blockers and then moves toward the antenna and out of bounds to use the blocker's hands.

Tennis Ball Throw

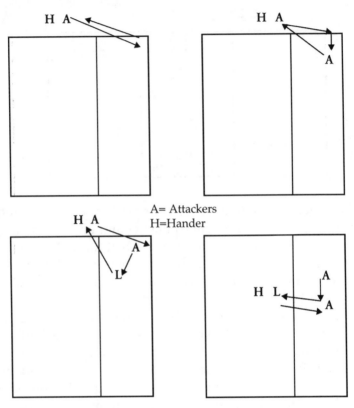

A= Attackers
H=Hander

This is a drill that is used a lot during our specialty practices. It is great for conditioning the arm swing of our attackers. It also helps the attacker with transition footwork patterns. It should be used for all three front-row attack positions. Start the drill by having a single attacker performing her attack approach with a tennis ball in her dominant hand and using the correct arm swing starting from the attack point behind the 3-meter line. After each approach, the attacker should transition back to the attack spot where she will be handed another ball and repeat the process. Be sure that the attacker is trying to throw the ball using the same arm action that she would in attacking the volleyball. She must keep her elbow high!

The next progression is to place the attacker at the net in a block start stance without any balls in her hands. This progression of the drill is trying to simulate more game-like circumstances for the attacker. The attacker blocks at the net and transitions off the net to the attack point, where she is handed a tennis ball by a teammate. The attacker then makes an approach and throws the ball into the opponent's court, then returns to her base defense position at the net. From there the attacker transitions off the net to play defense in the left front area, simulates digging a ball, and then transitions to her attack point outside the court to pick up another tennis ball. After attacking again, the attacker returns to her base defense position. From there the attacker uses a cross-hop footwork pattern to help block in the middle. After coming down from the block, the attacker transitions off the net to behind the 3-meter line, picks up a tennis ball, and attacks a "2" ball set.

Obviously, the drill can be adjusted according to which attacker is performing the drill. All you have to do is think about the movements that a particular position performs in a game.

Miss the Chair or Reverse Dodge Ball

	L L			
P				CH
	M M		C	CH
P		S		
	R R			CH

A great way to help your attacker avoid defenders in the opponent's court is to run this reverse dodge ball. The key to the drill is to miss the chairs that have been placed on the floor where your opponents normally place their defenders. In the preseason, we like to use this drill against all the various defenses that we will see throughout the season. Be sure to be realistic when placing the chairs on the floor, as most teams don't always have their personnel where they should be when they actually play defense.

Set the drill up with two primary passers in the backcourt, a setter at the net, and a couple of people in each of the attack areas. The coach will be located on the opposite side of the net to toss balls over the net to the passers. Instead of having the setter set balls in a predetermined order (i.e., left-middle-right), have the setter mix things up, which will keep the attackers on their toes. The attackers simply attempt to attack the ball into the opponent's backcourt in the open areas. The team must accomplish a predetermined number of attacks into the opponent's court without hitting the chairs. If you want to increase the area that the defense might cover try using pieces of carpet or padding.

A variation on this drill would be to place your players in their base defensive positions and have them work on free ball transition to attack. You can also work on your team's transition from defense to offense by placing a coach on a box, having the team defend the attack of the coach, and then transition to offense and miss the objects/defenders on the floor.

8

Transition Drills

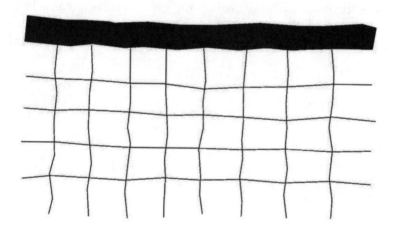

Baseball

This is a six-on-six scrimmage-type drill that has a great pace and helps the players to maintain a high level of intensity. It involves two teams playing six innings. Just like baseball, an inning consists of each team being allotted three outs per inning. Here's how it works:

Team A is the first team to "bat;" it gets to serve the ball at Team B. The server is allowed three outs. An out can be made if the server commits a service error or if the other team wins the rally. If the serving team wins the rally it is awarded a run/point and also gets to receive free balls from the coach until stopped by the defending team. The score for each team is the number of rallies it wins during the serve and the number of free ball rallies it wins. Once Team A has three outs, (it has lost three rallies during a serve), Team B gets to serve until it has three outs. The game is complete when both teams have accomplished all six rotations. The winner of the game is the team with the most cumulative runs/points at the end of the drill.

4-to-4 Cooperative-Competitive

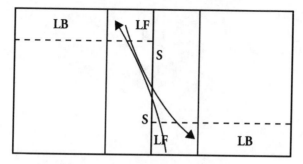

It is important that your left side attackers learn how to take advantage of open areas of the court that the block might provide you. This drill is a great way to develop your left side attacker's ability to hit hard crosscourt shots. The "4-to-4" in the drill title refers to zone 4 on your side of the net to zone 4 on the other side of the net. This drill is a cooperative-competitive drill in the fact that both sides are working together to keep the ball going and then at a designated point in the drill, it becomes competitive. At Indiana State, we had the ball cross the net three times, and then it becomes competitive. All the players in the drill call out "I-S-U" for the first three times the ball crosses the net, and then the attackers try to get the kill to win the drill.

This drill helps the left front and left back players work on their transition from their base defensive positions, to their rotated defensive position, to attack, and back to base defense again. It also helps the communication between the two players on each side.

3-vs.-3 Transition Drill

This is an intense, high-speed drill that forces the front-row players to think fast and move fast. It can also be a great conditioner! The goal of this drill is to work on the quick transition from offense to defense and vice versa. We typically play this drill to 3 points and a team earns a point when they have won two rallies in a row. The team that wins the rally gets to transition off the net and run a free ball offense.

Place a left front attacker, middle attacker, right front attacker, and a setter on each side of the net in their base defense positions. There should also be a coach-tosser on each side. The drill starts when the coach on the left side of the court slaps a ball, which is the cue for the players on his side to transition to the net to attack a free ball. The coach tosses the ball to the right front, and the attackers call out their desired set. The team on the right side of the net attempts to stop the other team's attack. We usually limit the types of attacks that the attacking team can use to make the drill fair to the defenders. Be sure to keep the drill moving at all times so that everyone is working on her transition footwork. Both teams should immediately return to their base defense positions regardless of who won the rally. The team receiving the free ball cannot release until the coach slaps the volleyball releasing the players for attack. The coaches can control the drill somewhat by how good of a free ball pass they decide to give their team. As a coach, try to make the drill as game-like as possible. Remember that all free balls don't always go directly to target. Make your players think on their feet!

Rapid-Fire Attack Series

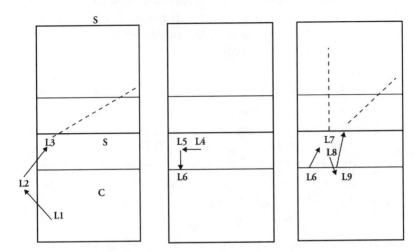

This drill is meant to simulate the quick pace that the player will experience during a game. It also forces the athlete to think fast and react to situations under pressure. For example purposes we will use a left side player that is a primary passer and will be having her play a man back defense. The primary purpose of this drill is to work on the player's transition speed and execution resulting in them attacking a number of different shots.

Here is the progression that the player will follow:

1. The player starts in the left wing passing position. A player at the opposite end line serves the ball at the player, who passes the ball to the setter.

2. After the pass, the player transitions to her attack point outside the court.

3. The setter sets a high outside ball to the player who must attack a hard 4-to-4 crosscourt shot.

4. After attacking the ball, the player transitions to her base defense position at the net to block.

5. From here, the player uses a cross-hop blocking footwork pattern to block a line shot by the opponent's right side attacker.

115

6. After the block, the player transitions off the net to an attack point at the attack line where it intersects with the sideline and then goes in for a 32 set and hits the ball to the 1/6 seam in the opponent's backcourt. The coach will toss a ball to the setter to simulate the ball being dug.

7. After attacking the ball, the player transitions into her base defense position at the net.

8. From here, the player transitions off the net to play defense in the left front area. The ball that the player digs comes from the setter who received one from the coach while the player was in her block stance.

9. After playing up the ball to the setter, the player must transition behind the attack line.

10. From here, the player attacks a 2 ball that is set by the setter.

This drill can be tailor-made for any position. All you have to do is think about the normal things that happen in a long rally and simulate these in the drill.

Side-Dee-Free

C

	L2			S	
		L1		L1	
		M2	M2		DS
	DS				
S		OP	OP	L2	

C

Side-Dee-Free means side out, defense, and free ball. This drill is a six-on-six game situation drill in which both teams are trying to accomplish a side out, then defense a free ball, and finally convert on free balls consecutively in order to rotate to the next rotation. The goal of the drill is to be the first team to get through all six rotations. Coaches need to locate themselves in the area outside the court in the right front area to toss free balls into play. Be sure to tell the players that they need to transition from one phase of the drill to the other and not stop to celebrate or sulk if they win or lose the rally in the first two parts of the drill. If the team that receives serve fails to win the first, second, or third phase of the Side-Dee-Free then it is a wash and the other team that won the rally gets the chance to receive the serve to make its attempt at accomplishing all three components of the drill. The drill creates a tough task that makes it necessary to concentrate for a prolonged period of time and creates sustained intense play in your team.

9

Serve Receive Drills

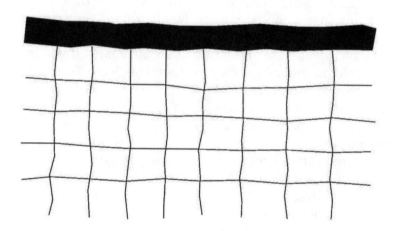

Around the World

	OP			
L2		OP		S
			DS	
DS		M2		
	M2			
L1		L1		
S			L2	

Team A   Team B

This is a drill that I thought of when one of my teams was stretching before practice, and I was playing the old basketball drill "around the world." If you recall, the drill involves shooting from various spots on the floor until you miss from one of the locations. You can "chance it" and take a second shot, but if you miss you return to the beginning. If you make the shot you continue to the next spot. This Serve Receive Drill was created using the same principle. Team "A" starts in the first serve-receive formation and is receiving serve from team "B." If team "A" is successful in siding out, it moves on to the second serve-receive pattern and continues through its rotations until completing all six rotations. The goal of the drill is to be the first team to get through all six rotations. If a team fails to side out on its first attempt it can choose to "chance it" and try to side out again, but it takes the risk of not siding out and going back to the start of the drill. If the team doesn't "chance it" the team can "stay" and give the other team a chance to go "around the world." This can be a very tough drill to finish unless you stack your first team against your second team.

First Kill Drill

This drill is used to help a team be successful with siding out on its first attack while receiving serve. It's a good drill to help your team in avoiding "runs" of points by opponents. In this drill we usually pit the first team against the second team. The goal of the drill is for the first team to get through all six serve-receive rotations by siding out on the first kill attempt for 7 of 10 serves. Once the first team has accomplished at least 7 side outs out of the 10 serves, it can rotate to the serve-receive pattern. If the first team fails to accomplish this, it must run three sets of sideline-to-sideline sprints.

A variation of the drill is to award two points for a "first kill" and one point for winning the rally even though the team didn't win the rally on the first kill. If you use this format, the first team must get to 12 points on 12 serves, which means it must get at least four first kills out of the 12 serves.

Challenge Serve-Receive

```
              T       T
    S  ┌──────────┬──┬──┬──────────┐  S
       │          │  │  │          │
       │    P1    │  │  │    P4    │
       │          │  │S │          │
    P2 │          │  └──┤    P5    │
       │          │S    │          │
       │    P3    │     │    P6    │
    S  │          │     │          │  S
       └──────────┴──┴──┴──────────┘
              T       T
```

The Challenge Serve-Receive Drill is meant to be a competitive exercise between all of your primary passers in which one group is trying to get 30 perfect passes before the other team of primary passers. The drill also helps your setters with their sets to the left front and right front area in addition to the serving accuracy of the servers.

Set up three primary passers on each side of the court along with a setter, two servers, and two targets for each setter. The primary passers will stay on the same side of the court until the second half of the drill when they will go to the other side of the net, but the servers and setters stay. Serves are alternated from one side to the other and the setters keep track of the perfect passes. The setter should only count passes as "perfect" if she feels that all three attack options can be run off of the pass. As mentioned before, the goal for the passers is to get to 30 perfect passes. The passers on each side should rotate between the left, middle, and right wing positions after 5 perfect passes so they are passing from every area of the court. The servers on each side are working for the passers on their side. They want to make it as difficult for the passers on the other side to get perfect passes as possible; however, for every service error that a server commits, the perfect passes of her primary passers are reduced by one. This forces the server to serve aggressively, but also smartly and efficiently.

Once a team has accomplished 30 perfect passes, it wins! Now it's time for the second half of the drill when the passers switch sides, but the servers and setters stay. This creates a situation where all the passers are passing balls from the different servers and both setters are setting balls from the different passers.

Serve-Receive Wash Drill

This drill involves two six-player teams competing against each other trying to get through all six of their serve-receive rotations with the highest number of points. A team must win two "little points," or rallies, in a row to get a "big point." The drill starts with team A receiving serve and team B serving and trying to defend. Team A will receive five served balls from team B. If team A wins the rally, it is awarded a "little point" and the players immediately transition into their base defensive positions. The coach slaps a ball and tosses the ball to team B, which must send over a free ball to team A. If team A wins that rally it gets another "little point," which gives it one "big point." If team B wins the free ball rally, then it is a wash. If team B won the rally that was initiated by its serve, it is awarded a "little point" and receives a free ball from team A. If team B wins the free ball rally it gets a second "little point" and is awarded a "big point."

Once team B has served five balls in that rotation, it receives five balls from team A, and the drill continues. The drill is complete when both teams have received serve in all six rotations. The winner of the drill is the team with the most "big points."

10

Team Offense Drills

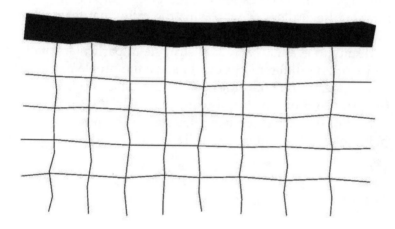

Rotation Battle Drill

	L1			
		L2		
				RS
DS			M2	
		M2	S	DS
		RS	L2	
	S		L1	

This drill consists of 6 games within one drill. The creation of this drill came about to help our team avoid having "bad rotations" where we would give up a number of points in a row. The drill involves having a 5-point rally game in each rotation. Regardless of who wins the rally, that team serves, but neither team rotates. This drill provides you with an opportunity to evaluate why you struggle in particular rotations and work on different options to solve the problem.

Set up teams on both sides and let the games begin! We play this drill to 5 points, but a team must win by 2 points. The winner of the drill is the team that has the highest cumulative point total at the end of the drill

Location-Weighted Scoring

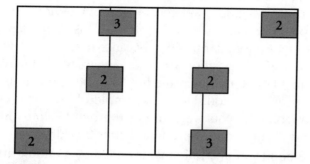

The location-weighted scoring drill was developed to help our team hit various spots on the floor that a particular opponent might leave open. We will tape off specific locations on both sides of the court, and if a team hits the ball into those locations it scores extra points on top of the one it scores by winning the rally. We will typically play the game to a higher score than a normal game due to the possibility of teams scoring multiple points by winning one rally. Try playing to 50 if you are playing rally to 30 in your regular games. I suggest making the two teams as even as possible so that everyone is challenged.

Position-Weighted Scoring

I'm sure there are times when we wished we had more options attack-wise and want to develop our options in a particular position, like the middle attack. This drill encourages setters to set a particular position because they will be awarded more points if that position scores on an attack. You may want to play to 40 or 50 points instead of 25 or 30 points due to the inflated scoring option. Here's a sample of how you can set up your points if you want to get the ball to your middles more and if you want to promote better blocking:

- 3 points for any rally that is ended by a middle attacker
- 2 points for any rally that is ended by a block
- All other rallies result in only one point.

Perimeter Point Scoring

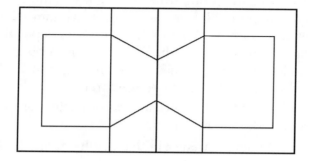

In this drill we utilize the same hourglass shape that we use in the Hourglass Attack Drill. While most defenses are considered perimeter defense drills, not all teams are consistent in staying on the perimeter of the court to play defense. The other thing you need to remember is that if you are playing against a team that puts up a good block, your attackers need to be able to cut around the block and still hit the ball in the court. This is a six-on-six full game drill in which both teams receive bonus points for scoring with shots that land in the perimeter or outside the hourglass shape on the floor. It takes time and effort to put the floor tape down, but having the tape on the floor gives the athletes a visual reminder of where to hit the ball, and it also helps your backcourt defenders to stay outside the block shadow and play defense where they should be on the floor. I suggest that you play rally games to 40 or 50 with perimeter points counting as 3 points and all other rallies counting as one point.

Situation-Weighted Scoring

The other weight scoring drill that we use is the Situation-Weighted Scoring Drill. It is also a six-on-six game-situation drill that we typically play to 40 or 50 points depending on how many bonus-point situations we have incorporated into the drill. Here are some of the bonus-point variations that we have used in the past that can be used in this drill:

- 2 or 3 points for service aces to promote more aggressive and accurate serving
- 2 or 3 points for any kill that results from a back-row attack.
- 2 or 3 points that result from a block to encourage the team to concentrate on blocking technique
- 2 or 3 points if the point scored is a result of running a combination play

Using a situation-weighted scoring format solves the problem of working on your problem areas within the framework of the game. It also encourages your setter to be more aggressive with her set selection, which will eventually make your offense more efficient.

11

Team Defense Drills

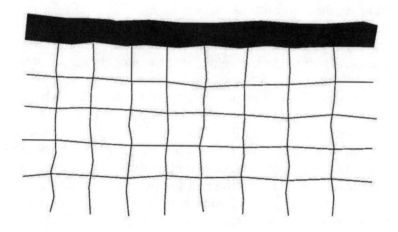

Mock Flow Drill

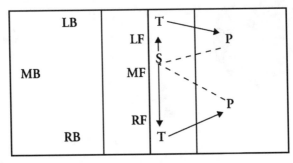

This drill is great for conditioning the legs of all your athletes. The backcourt participants get a nice workout for their legs due to all of the movement, and the middle blockers get the chance to move from pin to pin (antenna to antenna) and build on their endurance.

Set up your players in a full defense on one side of the court in their base defense positions. On the other side of the net you need two passers, a setter, and two targets for the setter. The drill starts when one of the targets tosses a ball to one of the passers. The passer passes the ball to the setter, who will set the ball either to the left front or right front target. As the setter sets the ball, the full defense on the other side of the net responds to the set and transitions to defend the attack. The block must get set and block before the ball reaches the target, who will overhead-pass the ball to one of the passers. As the ball is traveling from the target to the passer, the defensive players must get back to their base defense positions. The passer then passes the ball back to the setter, who will set the ball again, and the defensive team reacts accordingly. We will run the drill for one minute and then switch groups. Be sure that you conduct the drill using all of the defenses you typically use in competition.

Balance the Court

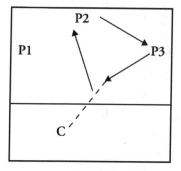 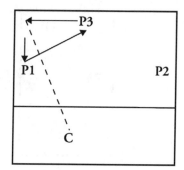

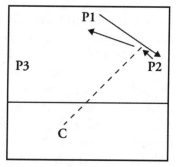

In this drill all three of your backcourt players must work together to cover the entire backcourt. If a ball is hit to an area of the court and one of the players must move away from her normal area of responsibility, then one of her teammates must move to cover that area. The player that moved to play the ball then continues the flow of the movement and replaces the player who is covering her area. This drill helps to balance the court out so there are not large open areas of the backcourt left undefended. It also helps your player understand the necessary adjustments to her platform to dig balls from various locations on the court. It also helps improves communication between the players and playing balls that are hit in the seams between defenders.

Around the World-Defensive Drill

	LB	L1		S L1	
DS		M2	M2		DS
S				L2	
		OP	OP		

Team A	Team B

This drill is similar to the Around the World Serve-Receive Drill in that it has the same principles of the Around the World basketball drill. A team has a "first chance" to win a rally; if it is not successful the team can "chance it" but if it fails on the second attempt, the other team gets an opportunity to go around the world. A team can "stay" if it chooses not to "chance it" but must relinquish the chance to go around the world to the other team and hope that the other team fails in its attempt. In the above diagram, team A is serving the ball and is trying to stop team B by using the defense. If team B sides out, team A can "chance it" and serve again in hopes that it can stop team B. If team A is successful, it gets to move to the next rotation and continue to serve the ball and play defense. If team A was not successful, team B gets the opportunity to serve and play defense to get through all six of the rotations and go "around the world." If team B is successful in stopping team A in its first three rotations and has failed on its first attempt in rotation four, it can choose to "stay" and let team A serve and play defense. If team B stops team A's attempt to go around the world, team B would start its next attempt in rotation four since it decided not to chance it the previous time. As was stated before, the first team to get through all six of rotations wins.

Switch

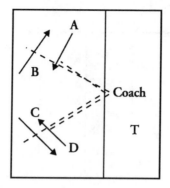

This drill is good to work on communication and foot speed. It involves two groups of two players and is designed to work on backcourt movement when balls are hit in the seam between two players. One group should involve a left front player and a left back player while the other group consists of a right front and right back player. The defenders need to be instructed that the player closest to the net always takes the path in front, while the player closest to the end line takes the deep route. This movement is called scissoring. The coach alternates to which group he hits between with both players in each group using the scissor movement to play the ball in the seam. If the ball is in front of the player that is closest to the net, she should play it and the deeper player should move behind to pick up the ball in case the front player decides not to take the ball or determines it is too deep to play. After the scissor movement is complete, the players simply switch positions until the next ball is attacked toward them.

All balls are being played to the target that is located in the right front area of the court. Once a group of two has accomplished 10 good digs to target, it is out and two more players hop into the drill.

Blind Ball

```
                    LF

  ┌──────────────┬──┬────────┬──────────┐
  │              │  │        │    S     │
  │              │  │  RF    │          │
  │   LB         │  │        │          │
  │              │  │        │          │
  │       MF     │  │  MF    │      MB  │
  │              │  │        │          │
  │   MB      S  │  │        │          │
  │              │  │  LF    │          │
  │       RF     │  │        │    LB    │
  └──────────────┴──┴────────┴──────────┘

       Team A                Team B
```

Many teams struggle because they don't play with anticipation. Do you find that your players simply react to what the other team does and is simply trying to keep up? This drill helps your athletes anticipate and also enhances their reaction skills. This is a six-on-six drill that simply involves a rally game to 30 points. Take a bed sheet and place it over the net so it covers about a fourth of the net. In the diagram above, the bed sheet has been placed over the net so that it is blocking the vision of the left side of team B's court and the right side of team A's court. When one team reaches 15 points, move the sheet to another location along the net. Things to emphasize for this drill are:

- Correct defensive positioning will put defenders in the best possible situations to dig balls that come from behind the sheet.

- Evaluating the flight of the ball and processing that information will help the defenders determine where the ball might go next.

- Concentrating on the movement of the players on the other side of the net will help the athletes anticipate what will happen.

- The players will dig more balls if they are using the correct staggered stance in their defensive play.

- The drill helps your team to play "out of system." They handle unusual circumstances on the court better if they learn how to improvise.

Pregame Warm-Up

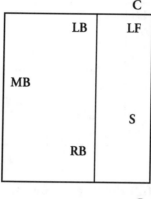

This is a common drill used by most collegiate volleyball pro-grams to warm up teams before a match. Place your setter in the right front to set balls to the coaches, who are located just off the court in the left and right front areas. Place defenders in the left front, left back, middle back, and right back areas. The setter is your right front defender. The coaches start the drill by slapping a ball and then attacking the ball to an area of the court that would be available in a game situation. Once a particular defender has successfully dug three balls to the setter, she should exit the drill and the next player in line steps into the drill. Be sure to place your right side players to set balls, also!

Full Defense vs. Three Hitters

	LB			OP	
		LF			
			S		C
MB		MF		M	
		RF			
	RB				

L

This drill pits a full defense against three attackers and a setter on the opposite side of the net. The drill is started by the coach who is tossing a ball to the setter on the hitter side of the court. This drill simulates a defense defending a free-ball attack and is meant to be a challenge for the defending team. The defending team must stop 5 balls before it is permitted to switch personnel. Of the five balls stopped, two must be with blocks and the other three can be by playing the ball up and converting against the three attackers who become blockers once the ball crosses the net from the attack. This drill is a great way for your blockers to work on locating their attackers, reading the setter's body postures, and fronting the attacker's attack routes.

12

Game Strategy Drills

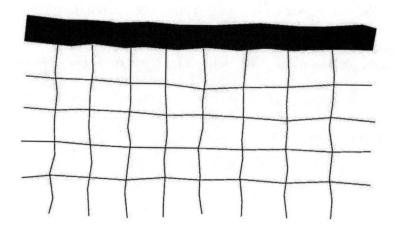

First to 10/First to 15

This drill has been a great exercise in helping our team get quick leads on our opponents at the beginning of every game. Getting out to an early lead, especially in rally scoring, can result in a huge edge. More importantly, avoiding the mistake of letting the other team start off with a big lead is addressed by this drill.

The premise of this drill is to have your team get to a certain point total before the team on the other side of the net. In this drill, it is best to pit your starting six against the second team. We always have a consequence in this drill for the loser. Typically, we have the losing team run 3 sideline-to-sideline sprints. Obviously, we use rally scoring in the drill since that is what we play on the collegiate level; however, the drill is just as effective using side-out scoring.

The starting six must get to 10 points before the second team gets to 5 points, and they must get to 15 points before the second team gets to 10 points. If the first team is successful in both phases of the drill, the second team runs. If the second team can get to 5 points before the first team gets to 10, or gets to 10 before the first team gets to 15, the first team runs. You can adjust the desired point levels to make the drill as difficult or as easy as you want.

Head to Head

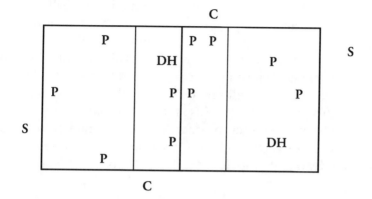

This is one of my favorite drills. It will help you find the players who can deal well with high pressure and produce when it comes down to crunch time. Head to head is a six-on-six drill, but you can also have extra players serving so everyone is involved if you have more than 12 on your squad. At the beginning of the drill you determine your "head to head" participants on each side of the net. These two players are the "go to" players for their respective sides. All sets must go to these players in order for their side to score points to win either a "small point" or a "big point." The goal of the drill is to be the first team to get to three "big points." In order to score a "big point" a team must achieve a "small point" by winning a rally that is started by receiving serve and siding out via an attack by the designated player on its side. If the players do this, they will immediately receive a free ball from a coach and they must win that rally by having the designated player on their side scoring the point; therefore, you have to win a rally by siding out and then win the next rally by converting on a free ball, and both rallies must be finished by the designated player. Obviously both teams know who the ball is going to at crunch time, and the designated player must produce against a team that knows where the ball is going to be set. This drill is also a great way to determine your team's depth chart by having players go head to head against each other. Another great way to conduct this drill is to have one of your left sides going head to head with one of your right sides so they are battling directly across the net in the drill.

Once you place people on the floor in the matchups you want, the players stay in those positions until the drill has a winner; therefore, there is no rotation. This allows all of the players to concentrate on perfecting their role in the drill. Make sure you are giving feedback to all of the drill participants, not just the designated players. Also remember that the designated hitter only has to be set in order to score a "little point" or a "big point." Anyone can be set if a team is defending against the other team's attempt to score its "little point" or "big point."

5-on-5 Adjust Drill

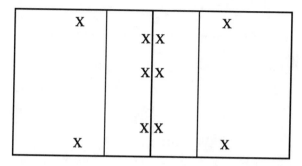

I came up with this drill to help my athletes think for themselves on the floor and not simply act like robots. In this drill, we place five players on each side of the net. We line up the teams except for the middle back position. We don't tell the teams to play a particular defense, but want them to figure out what their defensive positioning should be against their opponents. We simply play a rally game to 30 and see what adjustments the teams make to try to win the game. I have found that the athletes will start asking more questions about what they should do in certain circumstances. I don't know about you, but I love when athletes ask me questions as opposed to me just saying things to them.

Error Correction Drill

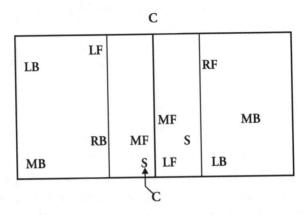

This is a quick-pace drill that is very game-like, but provides your players with the chance to immediately correct a problem that they have experienced. Set the drill up by putting two teams of six on the floor. Start the drill by having one team serve; as soon as someone makes a mistake that results in the end of a rally, a coach jumps onto the court and re-creates the situation in which the person that made the mistake had experienced. The coach gives quick feedback to the player as he/she is entering the court to re-create the situation. The coach quickly leaves the court and allows play to resume until another rally-ending mistake is made. Below you will find an example of how the drill works:

- The play starts with a serve and the receiving team passes the ball and sets; the left side attacker hits the ball into the block. A coach jumps onto the court and tosses a ball to the left side attacker to attack again. The rally continues.

- A right back player fails to dig a hard-driven spike from the opponent so the coach jumps onto the court and simulates the hard-driven attack and jumps off the court. The player digs the ball properly and the play continues.

- A blocker fails to penetrate on a block and the ball comes down between her and the net so a coach jumps onto the court and makes the blocker go up again and penetrate while the coach attacks the ball into the block. The ball is blocked back into the attacking team's side so the play and the drill continues.

Run the drill for a predetermined length of time. A variation on the drill is to replace the person who made the mistake with a player who is not in the drill. This can be fun for the teams when you end up with players playing in positions to which they are not accustomed, such as a defensive specialist playing in the middle or middles setting.

13

Miscellaneous Drills

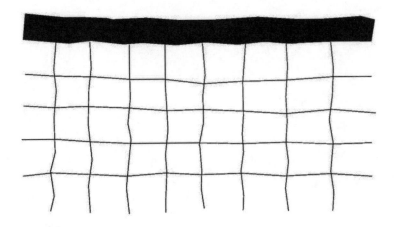

Player-Coach

I have found that one of the best ways to make your players better is to make them coach. I always encourage my athletes to coach youth volleyball teams if they can so they better understand the game and can self-evaluate themselves when they make mistakes.

If you are working on skills training, have the team partner up; have one partner performing the drill and the other partner acting as the personal coach. This helps the player with her analytical skills. Don't be shocked if you find that your players don't know as much as you thought they did or that they have trouble in figuring out what their teammates are doing wrong. The drill also helps the players to accept input from their teammates when it's offered in games and practices. Remember to have the players switch roles!

Rebounder

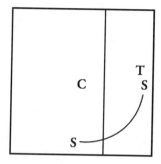

One of the best ways to change the momentum of a game is to turn a broken play or bad situation into a good one. This drill helps to make that happen if your setter receives a pass or dig in the net. This drill trains the setter to figure out how the ball will come out of the net. The rule of thumb is this, if the ball hits the net high by the net tape it will drop straight down, closer to the net. If the ball hits low in the net near the bottom it should pop out away from the net into the court.

The key to getting the ball out of the net is to be sure that your setter positions herself to the side of the ball with her hips and shoulders square to the sideline. The setter also should have her knees flexed and in a low stance. The setter should have her platform as flat as possible and parallel to the floor. Start by having the coach at an area just behind the attack line and throw a number of balls into the net at various spots along the net. At first have the setter try to forearm-pass every ball to the left front. After the setter has accomplished a certain level of success, have her try forearm-passing some 2 ball sets.